The Carmina
of Catullus

THE CARMINA OF CATULLUS

a verse translation

by Barriss Mills

1965

Purdue University Studies

144831

PREFACE

Do we need another verse translation of Catullus? Strictly speaking, perhaps, we do not. The roll-call of Catullus' translators is long and distinguished, as may be seen at a glance in Eleanor Shipley Duckett's *Catullus in English Poetry* or William A. Aiken's *The Poems of Catullus, Translated into English by Various Hands,* and a new version runs the double risk of being inferior to those that came before and also quite unnecessary.

But Catullus is a complex, many-sided poet—at once learned and lyrical, elegiac and colloquial, scurrilous and tender. His range is wide—from "little epics" in the manner of Kallimachos and Theokritos to brief personal lyrics like Sappho's and Archilochos' and the terse witty diatribes upon which Martial was to model his epigrams. His varying "moods" may occur alternately in a single poem. As a result, different translators have emphasized different aspects of his work, and these emphases sometimes tell us more about the translators' own predilections, and the verse "styles" of the times in which they wrote, than about Catullus' poetry itself. Richard Burton's version of the *Carmina,* for example, is as cranky and eccentric as anything that anti-Victorian Victorian gentleman ever wrote.

Even among recent translators there is great variation of "tone" and style. Horace Gregory's version stresses the soft, elegiac side of Catullus. We are given a somewhat callow young poet, disappointed in love and life and his friends. A *fin de siècle* mood emerges from Gregory's rather languid *vers libre.* Frank O. Copley's translation gives us an utterly different Catullus—much more manly

5

and vigorous, as quick and bright, intellectually, as Lesbia's sparrow, and ultra-modern. Style and mood are set by the use of colloquial English and even slang, and by echoes of nursery-rhymes, limericks, and popular songs.

A totally different approach to the *Carmina* may be seen in the recent translations by Louis and Celia Zukofsky. They seem to be trying to echo in English not only the meter but the actual sounds of the Latin in Catullus' lines. The opening line of carmen 51, "Ille mi par esse deo videtur," is turned into "He'll hie me, par *is* he? the Gods divide her," which is ingenious but harder to read than the original Latin and not like any English ever seen or heard elsewhere.

Most recent translators wisely abandon such attempts to reproduce the original meter and settle for some more familiar English verse form, whether rhyme and meter, as with Jack Lindsay and Roy Arthur Swanson, or unrhymed and unmetered cadences, as with Gregory, Copley, and Peter Whigham.

In the midst of all this, a new translation may hope to catch certain aspects of Catullus' thought and feeling and expression which others have missed or stressed insufficiently. My own strategy has been, first, to translate as literally as possible, with special regard for the connotations of the Latin and the sequences and juxtapositions of ideas and images, and then to shape the results into idiomatic English having some rhythmic value. If my version seems closer, at times, to prose than to any recognizable form of verse, that is of less concern to me than that it read like English we have heard, whether in verse or prose, and that it reflect as honestly as possible what seems to me to be the tone of the original. The most I can hope for, like any other translator, is that I have been more successful in some of the carmina than in others, and have caught certain aspects of Catullus' poetic genius better, here and there, than they have been caught before. There will never be a "final" translation of Catullus, or anybody else. But that is my justification for having undertaken another one.

My obligations to previous translators, and to scholars and critics, are so widespread that I shall not attempt to acknowledge them all. But I am particularly indebted to the prose translations of Walter K. Kelly and F. W. Cornish, to C. J. Fordyce's *Catullus: A Commentary,* and to H. A. J. Munro's *Criticisms and Elucidations of Catullus.* I want to thank Professors J. R. Himelick, William J. Roscelli, and Felix N. Stefanile, my colleagues in the Purdue English Department, for reading the manuscript. Many of their suggestions are incorporated in the text of my translation, though I have impertinently rejected others and must take full responsibility for whatever *gaucheries* still remain in it. My wife, Iola, who provided the sketches for this volume, helped me at all stages in the preparation of the book.

Finally, I must acknowledge the publication of several of the carmina, separately, in the following journals: *Approach, Bitterroot, Elizabeth, Exclusions, The Free Lance, The Goliards, the goodly co, Limbo, Midwest, Poetry Review, South and West, Sparrow, Trace,* and *The Wormwood Review.*

—Barriss Mills

West Lafayette, Indiana
March 31, 1965

THE POETRY OF CATULLUS

IN trying to describe Catullus' poetry, I must invoke that vague but useful word, "romantic." Some such term is needed to distinguish it from the work of more typically classical poets.

Vergil and Horace put us constantly in mind of the ideals of restraint, decorum, "distance," polish. For them the poem is a public thing, from its inception through its various "strategies" to the finished work on the page. It strives for "correctness" in thoughts and sentiments as well as diction and meter. Their poems are, in a sense, "official" poems—written, if not quite to order, yet with an eye to the expectations of the establishment. Theirs is laureate verse.

Reading Catullus, we have no such feeling. Restraint and decorum and distance are the last things his poetry suggests, and if there is polish, it is a polish that preserves the free forms into which experience naturally casts itself, rough edges and all. The source of Catullus' eternal freshness—his "modernity"—is this refusal to force the poem into conformity with traditional patterns. His best poems seem to have been thrown off in the heat of imagination, without regard for form.

I say "seem," for there is evidence that Catullus was as deliberately concerned with "craft" as those other poets, though he sought quite different effects. Carmen 50 tells of a day spent with Licinius, practicing various meters and verse forms for the sheer pleasure of it. Carmen 22, with its mingled scorn and pity for the poetaster Suffenus, shows how he felt about dilletantes in poetry. And half a dozen other poems demonstrate the vigor of his preferences in contemporary verse. Poetry, for Catullus, was no mere by-product of experience, or casual commentary upon it, but an art to which he was thoroughly committed—an art as important as anything else in life, and more important than most things.

Catullus' longer poems, especially, are "literary" in another sense as well. A number of them are imitations of older writers whom Catullus and his fellow-poets of the "new" school admired, especially the Greek poets of the Alexandrian group. Carmen 66 is a translation of Kallimachos' poem, "The Lock of Berenike," and carmen 64, which weaves together the marriage of Peleus and Thetis and the story of Theseus and Ariadne, is a "little epic" in the manner of Theokritos. Carmen 63, the Attis poem, is Catullus' contribution to the exploitation of the Cybele myth which the "new" poets seem to have set about quite deliberately as a counterweight to the "official" mythology of the Olympians. One can scarcely imagine a subject more romantic than the wild, self-mutilating frenzies of the Cybele cultists, unless it might be the Bacchantes, whom Catullus celebrates also, in carmen 64.

Like the Alexandrian poets, Catullus and his friends rejected the traditional epic out of hand. Catullus is quite explicit about that. Volusius' lengthy *Annals* are condemned in carmina 36 and 95, and in the second of these the brevity and presumably high polish (after nine years of work) of Cinna's *Zmyrna* is held up for favorable contrast. In carmen 35, Caecilius' unfinished Cybele poem is similarly praised.

But the longer, more literary poems, and the poems about poets and poetry, though they show most clearly his poetic affiliations and his concern for the poet's craft, are less characteristic of Catullus' poetic vitality and invention than the shorter, more personal ones. There is something a bit pedantic about the long, set pieces. They smell of the library and the literary circle. Though brilliantly done, they are in essence academic exercises. They earned him the epithet, "Docte Catullus," and they must have constituted a formidable battery of big guns for the defense of the "new" poets' position in the literary wars, but they are not the poems by which we best remember Catullus, once we put literary history and literary politics aside.

The best of the shorter poems seem more spontaneous and less programmatic. And by a kind of paradox which will be less surprising to poets than to scholars and critics, they are of more consequence, even historically, than the more self-consciously literary ones. "Docte Catullus"—the somewhat learned, somewhat antiquarian composer of poetic show-pieces and promoter of a poetic school—is a welcome counterbalance to the over-simplified image of Catullus as a "natural" poet, uttering his lyrical or angry or bawdy songs without forethought or art. But it is to the shorter poems, where Catullus forgets his "program" and his critical battles and his Cybele cult and strikes out for himself as an individual poet trusting his own eye and ear and sense of form, that we must look for the secret of his originality and his power.

Catullus' most characteristic form, in spite of his experiments with the longer poem, is the brief lyric—personal or satiric—written out of the mood of the moment. These poems have the effect of communicating the poet's strongest feelings and attitudes as directly and openly as possible. "Odi et amo," he says in carmen 85, and we are made acutely aware of his loves and hates throughout the *Carmina*. Whatever he likes, he likes intensely—without reservation or restraint. And his dislikes are equally violent. There is a kind of emotional "loyalty" at work here, forcing Catullus to take sides completely, for or against, and to scorn the middle ground of balanced judgments. There are no half-commitments, no qualified statements.

This applies especially to the Lesbia poems, where that loyalty is severely tried, and where Catullus is surprised to find, as he tells us in carmen 85, and also in carmina 72 and 75, that he can love and hate at the same time, after Lesbia has disillusioned him completely. But even here the love and hate do not cancel each other out. They exist, side by side, with undiminished intensity.

It applies also, less ambiguously, to his friendships and enmities among men, to his attacks on Julius Caesar and Caesar's political henchmen, and to his literary partisanship. Everything here is white or black, praise or blame, friend or enemy. There is something almost feminine about Catullus' trust in feeling rather than judgment and his loyalty to emotional commitments at any cost. Though he never "rationalizes" his prejudices (to do so might have seemed a disloyalty to them), he maintains them so consistently and stubbornly as to imply a kind of philosophical position—a trust of heart over head, of feeling over critical judgments and nice discriminations, of love and loyalty over temporizing and self-interest. If anyone ever wore his heart on his sleeve, Catullus did, and he seems to have expected the same of others—preferring the violent and even self-destructive commitments of an Ariadne or an Attis or a Laodamia to the cooler calculations of a Gellius or an Aufilena or a Caesar. Perhaps the reason he never completely rejects Lesbia is a realization that her growing promiscuity may have resulted from some emotional need beyond her control.

At times Catullus' emotionalism verges on hysteria. The alternation between joy and despair in his relations with Lesbia threatens, in carmen 76, to get out of hand, and we have an almost desperate searching for a way out of a crisis of "nerves"—a really black moment during which the will to live is flickering on the verge of going out. There is also a touch of the hysterical in Catullus' scurrilous denunciations of Julius Caesar and Mamurra, which seem to lack the saving wit and humor of his diatribes against rival poets and others whom he disliked. The case is especially puzzling because Caesar seems to have been on friendly terms with Catullus' father and to have offered, with his usual magnanimity, to patch up the quarrel with our poet, who refused. And yet, on the whole, Catullus' all-out emotionalism preserves a remarkable resiliency and healthiness of tone, as though there were inner reserves of strength which nothing could overcome.

Carmen 8, for instance, may be read as a healthy-minded version of carmen 76. In both poems Catallus tries to "steel" himself against the unfaithfulness of someone, presumably Lesbia, to whom he himself has remained true. But whereas in carmen 76 we feel the ground opening under him, the same sort of situation is treated lightly, even humorously, in carmen 8. Though the speaker pretends, in the last half of that poem, to feel sorry for the girl, as he names over the little attentions she will no longer receive from him, we know (and he knows) it is really himself he is sorry for. We know, as he knows, that the resolution to be firm will come to nothing, and that he will once again find himself pursuing the woman who has lost interest in him—the fool of love, ridiculous even in his own eyes, but somehow admirable in his submission to the fate of unwanted lovers.

To Horace, who wrote a famous poem upbraiding a young woman for taking her lover's mind off his military training, all this must have seemed quite unmanly, if not downright effeminate. We have come a long way from Homer's Achilles and Agamemnon quarreling over Briseis as though she were a prize horse; we are almost as far from Vergil's Aeneas, ruthlessly abandoning Dido in order to fulfill his heroic destiny. And we need only set Catullus' love poems over against Ovid's to bring into clearer perspective their unclassical qualities.

Ovid rings the changes on love and sex as insistently as does Catullus. His *Ars Amatoria* is a manual of the subject—a do-it-yourself kit for prospective philanderers of either sex. But compared with Catullus, Ovid's treatment of the subject is a bit cold and calculating—almost clinical. His theme is lust recollected (or anticipated) in tranquility —Don Juanism and connoisseurship in sex—whereas Catullus' is the heat of passion, or frustration, or disgust. We need not suppose that Catullus, anymore than Ovid, carried his writing tablets into the bedroom. But when he came to write the poem, it was more likely to take the form of immediate experience.

Probably Catullus' model for this sort of poem was Sappho. We know that carmen 51 is in part a translation from Sappho, and we may suppose he knew her other poems and carried them in his head as touchstones for his own poems of direct and immediate feeling. Perhaps he was similarly influenced by the poems of Archilochos, which he must have had the opportunity of reading in a less fragmentary state than that in which we know them. We do not find quite the same freshness and immediacy anywhere else in Greek poetry, except here and there in Theokritos' *Idylls,* and we do not find it in Latin poetry before Catullus.

When we look more closely at the peculiar effect of Catullus' best poems, the matter is not so simple as we might at first suppose. Each poem may seem a direct, rather naive outpouring of the feelings called up by the moment's encounter with experience. But the paradox of art—and particularly of an art like Catullus' (or Blake's, to invoke a comparison which is not so unlikely as it may seem)—is that the effects of freshness and immediacy are necessarily the result of deliberate craft.

Raw experience is always something of a muddle. The shape of the moment is always blurred: with one part of the mind we are thinking of something else. Even Joyce and other recorders of the stream-of-consciousness have had to impose arbitrary patterns on the complexity of our subjective impressions, and a more conventional report of experience must select one thread, or a very few threads, to be unraveled from the tangle. Classical art, like classical science, filters experience through a particularly fine screen. Irrational responses, or indecorous ones, are "censored" out. The result is not experience as it is lived and felt, but experience as it *ought* to be lived and felt, if we were reasonable creatures.

The danger of the classical strategy is creation of a convention of experience which is almost unrelated to the complexities of real life—or related to them only in an abstract way, much as classical science is related to the real complexities of nature. The "censor" has purged experience

away from us unnoticed and unremembered. The function of the poem, he might say, is to record, as sharply and vividly as possible, those moments when one is fully alive to the possibilities for happiness and sorrow. False dignity and self-pity are alike mistaken, and irrelevant to poetry.

Some such view of things accounts for the effectiveness of the famous poems about Lesbia's sparrow. The gaiety of carmen 2, in which we see Lesbia herself more vividly and charmingly than anywhere else — her playfulness, her teasing, and a kind of troubled sadness underneath—is balanced by the elegiac quality of carmen 3, on the death of that delightful bird. Together they are a perfect "parable" of the bittersweet brevity of pleasure and beauty and life itself. Nowhere else in literature, perhaps, do we find such a deft play of light and shadow, playfulness and seriousness, delight in the small lovelinesses of life and awareness of its inevitable end. I see nothing sentimental in these poems, for they are only nominally about Lesbia's sparrow. Their real subject is the essential human condition, seen unheroically and without solemnity or moralizing, but seen sharply and with a compassionateness which is given "distance" and form by the triviality of the ostensible subject. What Ecclesiastes said much more lugubriously, Catullus says without a hint of self-righteousness or self-pity.

Carmen 4, the poem about the little boat that brought Catullus home from his brief fling at imperialism in Bithynia, is a somewhat similar "parable." Cut from the living trees on the hill of Cytorus, bouncing lightly and quickly over the waves of the Black Sea and the Aegean and the Adriatic, it is laid up now by the shore of Lake Garda. It lived gaily, for awhile, and then it grew old and useless and died. What more can we say, of boats or men?

The kissing-poems, carmina 5 and 7, are in part sheer youthful boasting and exhuberance at the beginning of a love-affair. But even taken by themselves, they suggest a rather desperate gesture against the ravages of time, and in the context of the whole range of the Lesbia poems they take on still greater poignancy.

It is usually taken for granted that the Lesbia poems were written as a running account of a real love-affair with an older married woman named Clodia Pulcher. Arranged in a certain order, they can be made to show a rather neat progression from Catullus' first joy and surprise that Lesbia can love him in return (together with a certain amount of self-satisfaction in their having deceived her husband), through various stages of doubt and disillusionment about her faithfulness, to the final despair. But it is by no means certain they were written in so convenient an order, and it is altogether probable that Catullus' "moods" followed a somewhat less regular course. We shall probably never know just how "true" the poems are, in terms of a real-life love-affair. And it is of little consequence whether they are "true" or not, in that sense. What *is* important is the success with which they exploit the poetic possibilities of such a relationship.

Knowing as we do what a romantic poet like Keats could make of a rather stolid young lady named Fanny Brawne, and what Petrarch and Dante, in their different ways, made of Laura and Beatrice, we must hesitate to accept everything Catullus says about Lesbia and himself as a literal report. Lesbia may not be as elusive as Shakespeare's "woman colour'd ill," but it is doubtful that she is Clodia, or any other nymphomaniac Roman matron, transferred literally to the page. That there was a flesh-and-blood Lesbia, under whatever name, can scarcely be doubted. But we must assume that Catullus, like other poets before and since, made of her whatever he wanted to, for the poems' sakes. And what he makes of her, and of his love for her, is the most fascinating of all his "parables."

There are other women in the *Carmina:* Ipsithilla, who is sheer sexual fun and frolic; Ameana, "bankrupt Mamurra's whore;" Quintia, the girl with the handsome figure and little sex appeal; and Aufilena, tricky and quite immoral. But they serve chiefly to make Lesbia even more interesting by comparison. On the other hand there are the loyal loves of Acme and Septimius, and Laodamia and Protiselaus, and Thetis and Peleus, and the two marriage songs (carmina

61 and 62) to set off the vicissitudes of Catullus' affair with Lesbia. So wistfully does Catullus speak of these luckier lovers that we are almost persuaded he might have settled down with a less fascinating but less disturbing Roman *hausfrau*, if he had never met Lebsia. But that would almost certainly have deprived us of Catullus' poetry as we know it, and we must assume that his destiny or his muse had decreed for him a less comfortable but more romantic fate. As with Blake and Baudelaire, Catullus' poetry, and perhaps his personality, were nourished by emotional tension rather than repose.

In an ideal world, Lesbia might remain faithful, friends might not betray. Caesar and Mamurra might not usurp power, and Rome might not be overrun with pimps, prostitutes, pickpockets, and social climbers. We are conscious of such an ideal world behind the poems, and it occasionally appears in the foreground: in the poems about Catullus' beloved Sirmio, or his little farm, or his birthplace, Verona, where he goes to wait out the shock of his brother's death. But Catullus is no escapist, and it is Rome, the center of the brawling empire, where wealth and power sweep everything before them and bring every kind of sycophancy and perversion in their train, that he calls his "house and home," in carmen 68. He chooses to live and write his poems in that busy center of all the ambiguous activity of the time, quarreling with his enemies, showering love or good-natured abuse on his friends, and pursuing his elusive Lesbia.

And yet, living and writing in the midst of all the corruption and neuroticism of imperial Rome, Catullus remains somehow untouched by it. Something in his own nature insulates him from its contamination and buoys him up when it threatens to inundate him. Perhaps it is the "loyalty" we spoke of earlier, and perhaps that loyalty is to an ideal, of love and friendship and the essential goodness of life, which the shortcomings of human actuality cannot destroy. Perhaps he followed the Lesbia who might have been, while fully conscious of what the real Lesbia had become. He refuses to betray his own ideal of love and friendship, though others do, or to become cynical about human nature, *because* they do. He demonstrates a large charitableness toward life, with all its disappointments, and toward people, with all their faults.

In his poetry, which is all that finally concerns us, Catullus maintains a flexible and fluid tension between the romanticism of his own temperament and the harsher or more ludicrous realities of the human experience. Reality is not forced into conformity with his own ideal of love and loyalty; he sees clearly enough what the world is like, and what people are like. But neither is that ideal sacrificed to reality, in pessimism and despair. Through humor and the double consciousness, both worlds exist, side by side, playing upon one another with an almost inexhaustible energy and freshness. Life is worth living, on its own dubious terms, because loyalty and charity are still possible, however rarely they may be attained. And poetry is worth writing, on similar terms. We have warrant for that in the excitement we must always feel in reading the *Carmina*.

THE CARMINA OF CATULLUS

I

CVI dono lepidum novum libellum
arido modo pumice expolitum?
Corneli, tibi: namque tu solebas
meas esse aliquid putare nugas;
iam tum cum ausus es unus Italorum
omne aevum tribus explicare cartis
doctis, Iuppiter, et laboriosis:
quare habe tibi quidquid hoc libelli
qualecumque; quod, o patrona virgo,
plus uno maneat perenne saeclo.

1

To whom shall I dedicate
my pretty new book, freshly polished
with dry pumice stone?

To you, Cornelius,
for you used to think my trifles
might amount to something.

And you alone of the Italians
had the courage to write out
the whole history of the world
in three learned, painstaking
volumes, by Jupiter.

So take this little book,
such as it is, for whatever
it's worth. And may it
last, my muse and patroness,
more than a hundred years.

2

Sparrow, my sweetheart's pet,
whom she likes to play with, and holds
in her lap, and offers her fingertip,
and teases to bite sharply,
whenever my shining lady
is in the mood for fun.

I think that way she forgets
a deeper ache and finds respite
from her pain. I wish I
could play with you as she does,
and unburden my heart too
of its sadness and its cares.

2a

This is as great a joy to me
as was, they say, to that swift girl,
the golden apple that untied
her girdle, knotted up so long.

III

LVGETE, o Veneres Cupidinesque,
et quantum est hominum venustiorum.
passer mortuus est meae puellae,
passer, deliciae meae puellae,
quem plus illa oculis suis amabat:
nam mellitus erat suamque norat
ipsam tam bene quam puella matrem;
nec sese a gremio illius movebat,
sed circumsiliens modo huc modo illuc
ad solam dominam usque pipiabat.
qui nunc it per iter tenebricosum
illuc, unde negant redire quemquam.
at vobis male sit, malae tenebrae
Orci, quae omnia bella devoratis:
tam bellum mihi passerem abstulistis.
vae factum male! vae miselle passer!
tua nunc opera meae puellae
flendo turgiduli rubent ocelli.

3

Weep, Venuses and Cupids,
and all you gallant men.
My girl's sparrow is dead—
my sweetheart's pet sparrow
she loved more than her own eyes.

He was honey-sweet, and knew her
the way a girl knows her own mother.
He'd never leave her lap, but hopping
now this way and now that,
cheeped for his mistress alone.

But now he travels the dark road
from which they say nobody
returns. Evil take you,
evil shadows of Orcus,
who swallow up all lovely things.

Now you've taken him from me—
such a pretty sparrow. Cruel deed!
Poor little sparrow. It's for you
my sweetheart's eyes are red
and swollen with weeping.

4

That skiff you're looking at, friends,
claims she was once the fastest
of boats. No other timber
afloat could catch her, whether
pulled by oars or flying
under sail.

And this, she says, the threatening
Adriatic coast can't deny,
or the Islands of the Cyclades,
or famous Rhodes, or the wild
Propontis in Thrace,
or the dangerous gulf of Pontus,
where she who became a boat
was once a leafy wood. For there
on the hill of Cytorus she used
to whisper with talking leaves.

Pontic Amastris and boxwood-
bearing Cytorus, you knew
and know this, my skiff claims.
From her birth she stood on your heights,
she says, and first dipped oars
in your waters, and carried her master
from there through such violent straits,
whether the wind blew from starboard
or port or Jupiter came down
from both sides at once. She made
no vows to land-gods, sailing
from that far-away sea
here to this quiet lake.

But that's all over. Laid up now,
she grows old quietly
and dedicates herself to you,
twin Castor, and to you,
Castor's twin.

V

VIVAMVS, mea Lesbia, atque amemus,
rumoresque senum severiorum
omnes unius aestimemus assis.
soles occidere et redire possunt:
nobis cum semel occidit brevis lux,
nox est perpetua una dormienda.
da mi basia mille, deinde centum,
dein mille altera, dein secunda centum,
deinde usque altera mille, deinde centum.
dein, cum milia multa fecerimus,
conturbabimus illa, ne sciamus,
aut ne quis malus invidere possit,
cum tantum sciat esse basiorum.

5

Let's live and love, my Lesbia,
and value at a pennyworth
what the crabbed old folks say.

Suns may set and rise again,
but once our own brief light goes out,
night's one perpetual sleeping.

Give me a thousand kisses,
then a hundred, then another thousand.
Then a second hundred, and then
still another thousand, and then
a hundred more. And when
we've got to many thousands,
we'll lose count, till we don't know.

And spiteful persons won't be able
to put jinxes on us, unless
they know how many were our kisses.

6

Flavius, if your sweetheart
weren't uncouth and unpresentable,
you'd want to tell Catullus
about her. You couldn't hold your tongue.

I'll bet you're infatuated
with some hot little whore and ashamed
to admit it. You're not sleeping
alone nights. It's no use
keeping quiet about it. Your bed,
decorated with flowers and smelling
of Syrian oil, and the sheets
rumpled everywhere, on both sides,
and the whole thing still creaking
and shaking—they give you away.

Yet you go on stubbornly
keeping silent. Why? Your body
wouldn't be worn crooked unless
you were up to some debauchery.

Whatever it is, good or bad,
tell me about it. I'll publish
you and your lady-love
to the skies in my witty verses.

7

You ask how many kisses, Lesbia,
would satisfy and surfeit me.
As many as the Libyan sands that lie
in spice-bearing Cyrene, between
Jove's burning oracle and old Battus'
holy tomb. Or as many as the stars
that look down from the silent night
on mankind's secret love-making.
Kissing you that many kisses
would satisfy and more than satisfy
your mad Catullus—kisses
beyond the counting of the curious
and bewitchment of evil tongues.

8

Wretched Catullus, stop moping.
Face it. What's gone is gone.
The bright days used to shine
for you when you'd follow that girl
wherever she went, and we loved her
as no one will ever be loved
again. Then every kind of fun
you wanted was granted, and the girl
didn't say no. The bright days
really shone for you then.

Now she's not interested
anymore, and since there's nothing
you can do about it, you should be
indifferent too, and not go chasing
after one who avoids you, making
your life a misery. Stiffen
your mind. Be unyielding, hard as stone.

Goodbye, girl. You'll find Catullus
hard as stone. He won't be running
after you anymore or asking
for anything you don't want to give.
But you'll be sorry, wicked girl,
when night after night no one asks you.

What sort of life will that leave you?
Who'll be coming to see you now?
Who'll tell you you're pretty? Whom
will you love? Who'll call you his?
Who'll get your kisses? Whose lips
will you bite? But you, Catullus,
be unyielding, hard as stone.

9

Varanius, best of all my friends
in a radius of three hundred miles,
have you come home again to your
own fireside and your dear brothers
and aged mother? Yes, you've come
and that's welcome news to me.
I'll get to see you safe and sound
and hear you tell about Spain—
country, people, the latest doings—
as you always do. And I'll hug you
and kiss your sweet mouth and eyes.
Which one of you, all you happy men,
is happier or luckier than I?

10

Varus picked me up at the Forum,
where I was killing time, to go see
his girl friend. Not bad looking,
I could see at a glance—a stylish
little piece. After we'd gone in,
we got to talking about this
and that, and for one thing,
what Bithynia's like nowdays,
and how everything's going there,
and whether there'd been any
money in it for me.

I told them the way it was—
how no one, myself or the praetors
or their staffs, managed to come home
better-heeled—especially us,
since our praetor was a bastard
who didn't give a damn for his staff.
"Well, at least," they said, "you must
have got hold of some slaves to carry
your litter, since that's the place
they're supposed to come from." And I,
wanting to make myself out
to the girl as someone that's not
too badly off, said "No,
the province I was assigned to
was bad enough, but it wasn't
so hopeless I couldn't provide myself
with eight strong-backed fellows." Of course
I hadn't even one, anywhere,
strong enough to heave the broken leg
of an old bed onto his shoulder.

Then, like the little bitch she was,
she said "My dear Catullus,
please, lend me the use of them
for a bit. I want to be carried
to the temple of Serapis."
"Wait," I told the girl. "What I said
just now about their belonging
to me—I got it wrong.
A friend of mine—it's Gaius Cinna—
he bought them for himself. But what's
the difference, really, whether
they're his or mine. I use them
just the same as if I'd bought them
for myself. But with a silly thing
like you—so stupid and troublesome—
a man doesn't dare speak carelessly."

11

Furius and Aurelius,
Catullus' companions, whether
he goes among the farthest Indians,
where the shore beats with the far-
resounding eastern wave, or among
the Hyrcanians and soft Arabs,
or the Sacae or the Parthians,
carrying their bows and arrows.

Or where the seven-mouthed Nile
colors the sea. Or when he plods
over the high Alps, visiting
mighty Caesar's monuments—
the Gaulish Rhine or the terrible
Britons, farthest away.

Ready to brave all these
and whatever else the gods' will
may bring, please carry to my girl
these few unhappy words.

Tell her to live happy
with her lovers—all three hundred
she makes love with all together
but loves none of them truly,
wearing them all out the same.

Tell her not to pay any attention
to my love, as she used to do,
for thanks to her it has fallen
like a flower on the edge of the field
touched by the plow passing by.

12

These left-handed tricks you play
when we're all joking and drinking
aren't cute, Asinius
Marrucinus. Stealing handkerchiefs
when people aren't looking—if you think
that's funny, you're wrong, you idiot.
A stupid trick—not a bit clever.

If you don't believe me, ask
your brother Pollio.
He'd be delighted to redeem
your thieveries—even at the cost
of a whole talent. There's a boy
who's the last word in manners and fun.

So be prepared for three hundred
hendecasyllables—or return
my handkerchief. What bothers me
isn't the price but the fact
it's a keepsake from my friend.

Fabullus and Veranius
sent me handkerchiefs as gifts
from Setabis in Spain.
And naturally I treasure them
as I do my friends Veranius
and Fabullus.

XIII

CENABIS bene, mi Fabulle, apud me
paucis, si tibi di favent, diebus,
si tecum attuleris bonam atque magnam
cenam, non sine candida puella
et vino et sale et omnibus cachinnis.
haec si, inquam, attuleris, venuste noster,
cenabis bene: nam tui Catulli
plenus sacculus est aranearum.
sed contra accipies meros amores
seu quid suavius elegantiusve est:
nam unguentum dabo, quod meae puellae
donarunt Veneres Cupidinesque,
quod tu cum olfacies, deos rogabis,
totum ut te faciant, Fabulle, nasum.

13

You'll dine well at my house
one of these days, my dear Fabullus,
the gods willing, if you'll bring
a good dinner with you,
and plenty of it—not forgetting
a pretty girl, and wine and wit
and laughter of all sorts.

If, as I say, you'll bring
all this, my charming friend,
you'll dine well. For your Catullus'
purse is full—of cobwebs.

Nevertheless, you'll receive
the essence of true love
or something sweeter and finer,
if that's possible. For I'll give you
a perfume the Venuses and Cupids
presented to my girl. And when
you smell it, Fabullus,
you'll beg the gods to make you
all nose!

14

If I didn't love you more
than my eyes, dearest Calvus,
I'd hate you, the way everyone
hates Vatinius, for this present
of yours. What did I do?
What have I said? Why
should you inflict upon me
all these miserable poets?
May the gods rain evils upon
that client of yours who sent you
such a collection of villains.

But if it was Sulla the critic,
as I suspect, who gave you
this "newly discovered" gift,
then I'm not angry but delighted.
You got just what you deserved!

My god, what a frightening
damned book! To think that this
is what you sent your Catullus
to kill him off all at once
on the day of the Saturnalia,
my favorite holiday.
No, no, you rascal, this isn't
the last you'll hear of it.

If morning ever comes, I'll run
to the bookseller's shop and gather
together all the Caesii,
and the Aquini, and Suffenus,
and all sorts of similar
nauseating stuff,
to repay you with such tortures.

Meanwhile, goodbye—be off
to wherever you dragged your dirty
feet from, you curses of the age—
you worst of all possible poets.

14a (Fragment)

If there happen to be any readers
of my nonsense who aren't afraid
to touch me with your hands. . . .

15

Aurelius, I'm entrusting
myself and my love to you.
And I'm asking a small favor:
if ever, with all your heart,
you longed to keep anything
pure and unspoiled, you'll protect
my modest boy—and I'm not talking
about the general public.

I'm not worried about the nobodies
going by here and there in the streets,
busy with their own affairs.
To tell the truth, it's you
I'm afraid of, and that lechery
of yours that's so dangerous
to boys, good and bad alike.

Indulge it however you please,
on whomever you like, as often
as you're capable of—somewhere else.
I make this one exception,
not unreasonably, it seems to me.

But if your degenerate mind
and insane passion should impel you
to so great a crime—such wickedness
as inciting treason against *me*—
then you're in for the terrible fate
of adulterers: feet tied—
back door wide open—run through
with radishes and mullets.

16

Frig you, Aurelius
and Furius, you crazy perverts.
You accuse me of impropriety
just because a few of my verses
are a bit overripe. A poet's
life, if he's dedicated,
ought to be pure, but not
necessarily his verses.

On the contrary, they owe
their wit and charm to being
racy and improper enough
to stir up the libido—
and I don't mean only in boys,
but in graybeards, too, unable
to limber up their frozen loins.

But you, when you read about
so many thousands of kisses,
make up your minds I'm effeminate.
Frig you, my friends.

17

Colonia town, you'd like to hold
your festivals on a long bridge,
and you're all ready for the dancing
to begin, but you don't quite trust
the crazy legs of your small bridge,
teetering on its second-hand piles,
for fear it will come tumbling down
and lie on its back in the mud.

I hope you'll get your new bridge
made just the way you want it—
one upon which the holy rites
of Salisubsilus himself
might be performed—if you'll grant me
this gift, Colonia,
to make me laugh my loudest.

There's a townsman of mine I'd like
to see pitched head over heels
into the mud from your bridge—
right into the deepest, blackest
part of the whole stinking,
muddy lake. The man's
an utter fool. He hasn't
the sense of a two-year-old baby
rocked to sleep in his father's arms.

His wife's a girl in the first flower
of youth—a girl more delicious
than the tenderest kid, who ought
to be guarded more carefully
than the ripest grapes—and he lets her
play around as much as she likes
and doesn't give a damn.

And he never bestirs himself
on his own part, but lies there
just like an alder in the ditch
cut down by a Ligurian axe,
with about as much perception
as if she didn't exist.
Just so, this booby of mine
sees nothing, hears nothing.
He doesn't even know who he is
or whether he's alive or not.

He's the fellow I want to send
headfirst from your bridge, to see
whether after all it's possible
to wake up the stupid sluggard
and get him to leave his sprawling mind
behind in the stinking mud,
the way a mule loses her iron
shoe in the sticky mire.

21

Aurelius, you begetter
of starvations—not only
these but all that ever were,
or are, or are going to be
in years to come—you're trying
to seduce the boy I love.
There's nothing secret about it.
You're always where he is,
cracking jokes, sticking by his side,
trying everything. It's no use.
While you're still plotting against me,
I'll beat you to it. Still,
if you did it on a full belly,
I'd never say a word. The thing
that really annoys me is this:
you'll teach my boy to go hungry
and thirsty. Stop, while you decently
can, or I'll finish you off
disgracefully.

22

That fellow Suffenus—
you know him, Varus, pretty well—
is a likable person, a good talker,
well mannered. And he turns out
more verses than anyone else.
He must have written ten thousand
or more—not just scribbled down,
in the usual way, on old scraps
of parchment. With him
it's the best paper, brand new rolls,
and new bosses and ribbons
and wrappers, all ruled with lead
and polished with pumice stone.

But when you read them, you'd imagine
that same charming, well-bred Suffenus
was a goatherd or a ditchdigger,
the change is so shocking. How come?
The same fellow who resembled
a regular court jester
just now, or something cleverer,
if that's possible, turns stupider
than the stupidest country oaf
as soon as he attempts a poem.

And yet he's never so happy
as when he's writing one of them—
he's so pleased with himself, and admires
himself so much. But of course
we all fool ourselves the same way,
and there's no one who isn't a Suffenus
somehow or other. Each one of us
is allotted his own brand of foolishness.
But we never look into the knapsack
of nonsense on our own back.

23

Furius, you haven't
a slave or a moneybox,
or a bug or a spider or a fire.
But you've a father and stepmother
whose teeth can chew up stones.
And you're happy with your father
and that dried up stick of wood,
your father's wife. And no wonder.

You're all in the best of health,
your digestions are excellent,
and you haven't a thing to worry about—
fires or earthquakes or robberies
or poison plots or any other
dangerous threats. And besides,
your bodies are drier than bone,
if anything can be drier,
from the sun and cold and hunger.

How could you help being well
and happy? You're free of sweat,
free of saliva and mucous
and nasty running noses.
Add to this cleanliness
a greater one: your backsides
are cleaner than a saltcellar,
for your bowels don't move ten times
in a whole year, and even then
it's harder than a bean or a pebble,
and if you rub it and polish it
in your hands, you won't even get
a finger dirty. Don't despise
such blessings or belittle them,

Furius. And don't go on begging
for a hundred sesterces. You're
happy enough already.

24

Young flower of the Juventii,
past, present, or to come,
I'd rather you'd give Midas' money
to that fellow who has neither
a slave nor a moneybox,
than allow him to make love to you.

"What? Isn't he a handsome man?"
you'll say. And so he is.
But this fine fellow has neither
a slave nor a moneybox.

Ignore it, make light of it,
if you will, but still he hasn't
a slave or a moneybox.

25

Girlish Thallus, you're softer
than rabbit's fur or goose down,
or an eartip, or even an old
dusty spiderweb—and yet
more rapacious than a raging storm
or those divine bird-women
who swoop down with gaping mouths.

Give me back the cloak you stole,
and my handkerchiefs from Setabis,
and my ancient Bithynian pictures,
which you keep on display, you idiot,
as though they were heirlooms.

Unglue them from your fingernails
and let go of them right away,
or the burning whip will inscribe
ugly lines on your tender bottom
and soft little hands, and you'll toss
like a small boat caught in an angry
wind on the vast sea.

XXVI

FVRI, villula nostra non ad Austri
flatus opposita est neque ad Favoni
nec saevi Boreae aut Apheliotae,
verum ad milia quindecim et ducentos.
o ventum horribilem atque pestilentem.

26

My little country place, Furius,
isn't exposed to the south wind,
or the west, or the savage north wind,
or a wind from the east. Instead,
it's exposed to the ruinous blast
of a mortgage of fifteen thousand
two hundred sesterces—a damned
unpleasant situation.

27

You boy there, serving
the old Falernian, bring me
the straight stuff after this.
Those were Postumia's orders—
our hostess, who's drunker
than the drunkest grape.
Skip the water. Water
kills wine. Take it away
somewhere, anywhere.
Give it to the teetotallers.
This is the juice of the god!

28

You followers of Piso—
an empty-handed crew,
with duffels always at the ready
and easily transportable—
good friend Veranius
and you, my Fabullus,
how's it going with you?
Have you had your fill by now
of freezing and starvation
with that scum? Do your budgets
show a slight balance on the debit side,
as mine did, after I'd followed
my praetor and wound up in the red?

O Memmius, you really
gave me the shaft in that affair.
And as nearly as I can see,
you fellows are in a similar fix—
screwed by the same kind of bastard.
No more of this chasing after
influential acquaintances!
But may the gods and goddesses
load you with curses, Piso
and Memmius, you blots
on the lineage of Romulus and Remus.

29

Who can be aware of this
and put up with it, unless
he's shameless himself—a swine
and a swindler? This Mammura's
got his hands on all the riches
there ever were in long-haired Gaul
and farthest Britain.

Effeminate Caesar, will you
continue to be aware of this
and put up with it? If so,
you *are* a shameless swine
and a swindler. And now,
full of pride and running over
with graft, will he go sauntering
through everyone's beds, like a white
cock pigeon or an Adonis?

Effeminate Caesar, if you
continue to be aware of this
and put up with it, you're a shameless
swine and a swindler. Was it this
that took you, our best general,
to the farthest island of the west—
so this worn-out lecher of yours
can squander twenty or thirty
million sesterces? That's
a queer kind of generosity.
Hasn't he squandered enough
and guzzled enough already?

First it was his patrimony
down the drain, and then his spoils
from Pontus, and next the loot
from Spain, which the gold-bearing
Tagus River gives witness of.
And now the Gauls and Britons
are expecting the worst. Why favor
that scoundrel? What's he good for
except swallowing up any money
that comes to him? Was it for this,
all-powerful father- and son-in-law,
you laid waste to all the world.

30

Ungrateful Alfenus,
false to your true companions,
haven't you any pity,
cruel one, for your dear friend?
Don't you feel any compunction
about betraying me, deceiving me,
faithless one? Do the wicked deeds
of deceitful men find favor
with the gods? But you utterly
disregard all this and abandon me
in my misfortune. Tell me,
what are men to do, and whom
can they trust? You yourself
used to tell me to surrender my soul
to you, unjust one, leading me
into love as though everything
were safe for me. But now
you draw back from me and let
the winds and the cloudy air
blow away your lying words
and actions. If you've forgotten,
the gods still remember. Faith
remembers, and will make you
sorry, some day, for what you've done.

XXXI

PAENINSULARUM, Sirmio, insularumque
ocelle, quascumque in liquentibus stagnis
marique vasto fert uterque Neptunus,
quam te libenter quamque laetus inviso,
vix mi ipse credens Thyniam atque Bithynos
liquisse campos et videre te in tuto.
o quid solutis est beatius curis,
cum mens onus reponit, ac peregrino
labore fessi venimus larem ad nostrum
desideratoque acquiescimus lecto?
hoc est, quod unum est pro laboribus tantis.
salve, o venusta Sirmio, atque ero gaude:
gaudete vosque, o Lydiae lacus undae;
ridete, quidquid est domi cachinnorum.

31

Sirmio, dear little eye
of all the islands and peninsulas
which both the Neptunes carry,
in quiet lakes and on the vast sea—
how willingly and joyfully
I come back to you, scarcely able
to believe that I've left Thynia
and the plains of Bithynia
to see you safely again.

What can there be more blessed
than to put aside all worry
when the mind lays down its burden,
and tired from the hardships of travel,
we come home to rest on the bed
we've longed for? This alone
repays us for all our troubles.

Welcome, beautiful Sirmio.
Rejoice with your master. And you,
waters of the Lydian lake,
rejoice, and laugh out loud
with all your watery laughter.

32

My darling, delicious,
delightful little piece, Ipsithilla,
I love you. Invite me to come
spend the noon siesta with you.
But if you do, see to it
that nobody leaves the door locked,
and don't take it into your little
head to go out somewhere
for a minute. Stay at home
and get yourself ready for nine
uninterrupted bouts of love.
If it's all right, call me quickly,
for I'm lying here now on my back,
stuffed full of lunch and bursting
through my underclothes and even
my outer clothing.

33

Notable among the crooks
in the public bathing-places—
you, father Vibennius,
and your effeminate son.
Father's cleverer with his hands
and Junior with his voracious
tail. Why don't you both
banish yourselves to hell,
since pappa's thieving's common
knowledge, and you, sonny-boy,
can't peddle your hairy buttocks
around here any more?

34

We are virgin girls and boys
protected by Diana.
Let us sing to Diana,
innocent boys and girls.

Daughter of Latonia,
great child of greatest Jove,
born by her mother under
the Delian olive-tree,

to become the patroness
of mountains and green woods
and unfrequented valleys
and resounding rivers.

Called Juno of Childbirth
by mothers in labor, and Goddess
of the Crossroads, and Luna
of the deceitful light.

Measuring the year, goddess,
with your monthly circuitings,
you fill up the country barns
of the farmers with rich harvests.

Holy by whatever name
you prefer, shield the people
of Romulus with your kind graces
as you've done from the earliest times.

35

Paper, go tell that love poet,
my old friend Caecilius,
to come to Verona, leaving
behind the walls of New Comum
and the shores of Lake Larius.
I want him to take a look
at certain cogitations
of a friend of his and mine.

If he's wise, then, he'll chew up
the roads, even if that lovely
girl of his calls him back
a thousand times, and throws
her arms around his neck,
and pleads with him to stay.
The girl's madly in love with him,
if my information is correct.

Ever since she read the beginning
of his poem to Cybele—
from that very moment the fires
have been eating up the poor girl's
insides. I don't blame you,
a girl more learned than Sappho's
Muse, for certainly Caecilius
has got off to an excellent start
in his ode to the Great Mother.

36

Volusius's Annals,
you'd make fine toilet paper—
but carry out a vow for my girl.

She promised holy Venus
and Cupid if I came back to her
and stopped threatening to unleash
my bad-tempered iambics,
she'd give to the slow-footed god
a prime example of the scribblings
of the worst poet she could find,
to be burned with unlucky wood.
And now my girl's discovered
those worst of all possible poems
she jokingly promised the gods.

You whom the blue sea bore,
who live in sacred Idalium
and the plains of Urios
and Ancona and reedy Cnidus
and Amathus and Golgi
and Durachium, the guest-house
of the Adriatic—record
the vow as duly received
and paid, if it isn't *too* stupid
and ugly. Into the fire
you go, this bundle of cloddishness
and witlessness—Volusius's
Annals—excellent toilet paper.

37

Disreputable tavern, and you gang
who hang out in it, behind
the ninth pillar from the temple
of Castor and Pollux—do you think
you're the only fellows with the right
to tumble all the pretty girls,
and the rest of us are nothing
but goats? Just because you sit
together there like dummies,
a hundred or two, don't think
I can't tackle all two hundred
at a sitting. Believe me,
I'll scribble your names and epithets
all over the front of the place.

For my girl's run out on me—
the one I loved more than anyone
will ever be loved, and for whom
I've fought great wars—and come
to stay there. Now all you fine,
noble fellows make love to her,
and what's even more shameful, every
small-time lecher from the back streets
and alleyways. You above all,
long-haired Egnatius—spawn
of a Spanish rabbit-warren,
whose only claim to distinction
is a bushy beard and teeth
scrubbed with Spanish urine.

XXXVIII

MALEST, Cornifici, tuo Catullo,
malest, me hercule, et laboriose,
et magis magis in dies et horas.
quem tu, quod minimum facillimumque est,
qua solatus es allocutione?
irascor tibi. sic meos amores?
paulum quid lubet allocutionis,
maestius lacrimis Simonideis.

38

Your Catullus isn't well,
Cornificius. He's sick,
by Hercules, and in trouble,
getting worse by the day and hour.
But you—though it's the simplest
and easiest thing in the world—
haven't said a word to comfort him.
I'm angry with you. Is this
the way to treat a good friend?
A word or two would be something,
or a tear, as sad or sadder
than Simonides' verses.

39

Because he has bright, white teeth,
Egnatius is always grinning.
If he shows up in the courtroom
just as the lawyer for the defense
is moving everybody to tears—
he grins. Or if people are mourning
beside the funeral pyre
of a dutiful son—at the moment
the heartbroken mother begins
to cry—he grins. Whatever
the occasion—wherever he is
and whatever he's doing—he grins.
It's a disease he's got,
and in my opinion it's neither
appropriate nor attractive.

And so, a word of advice
from me, good Egnatius.
Even if you were a Roman
or a Sabine or Tiburtine
or a piggish Umbrian
or a round-bellied Etruscan
or black, toothy Lanuvian
or a Transpadene (to touch
on my own people) or anyone
at all who cleans his teeth
with clear water—even then
I'd urge you not to be always
grinning. Nothing's sillier
than meaningless laughter.

But you're a Spaniard,
and it's an old Spanish custom
whenever you make water, to keep it
overnight to brush your teeth
and red gums with. Therefore,
the better polished your teeth are,
the more publicly you proclaim
you've been drinking piss.

40

What insanity, poor Ravidus,
drives you headlong into the path
of my iambics? What god,
invoked in an evil hour,
inspires you to stir up
this senseless quarrel? Or is it
simply that you want to get yourself
talked about? What are you after?
Are you trying to become notorious,
no matter how? Well, you will,
since you've decided to make love
to my sweetheart and endure
my everlasting revenge.

41

Ameana, that worn-out slut,
had the nerve to proposition me
to the tune of ten thousand sesterces—
that girl with the ugly nose,
bankrupt Mamurra's whore.

You relatives that look after
the girl, call in the doctors
and your friends. She's out of her mind
or else she's forgotten to take
a look at herself in the mirror.

42

Come, hendecasyllables—
all there are of you, anywhere
in the world. An ugly whore
is trying to make a fool of me.
Believe it or not, she refuses
to give me back my writing tablets.
Let's go after her and demand them
back again. Who is she,
you ask? The one you see there
mincing along—grinning
like a cheap comedian,
with a mouth like a Gallic terrier.

Close in on her and demand them
back again: "Dirty whore,
give back the writing tablets.
Give back the writing tablets,
you dirty whore." You don't
even care? You piece of filth,
you strumpet, or even worse,
it that's possible.

But you needn't think
this is the end of it.
If nothing else can be done,
let's force a blush on that brazen
dog's face. Call out again
even louder: "Dirty whore,
give back the writing tablets.
Give back the writing tablets,
you dirty whore." But we're
not getting anywhere. Nothing
fazes her. You'd better
change your tactics, and see
if that works any better:
"Chaste virgin, won't you kindly
give me back my writing tablets."

43

Greetings, girl. You've neither
a small nose or a pretty foot
or black eyes or long fingers
or a dry mouth or even
an especially refined tongue.
Bankrupt Mamurra's mistress—
is it you the Province calls
beautiful? Is it you
they compare my Lesbia to?
My god, what an idiotic,
undiscriminating age!

44

My farm, whether you're Sabine
or Tiburtine (for they claim
you're Tiburtine—the ones
who don't take pleasure in annoying
Catullus; but the ones who do
will bet anything you're Sabine)—
anyway, whether you're Sabine
or more properly Tiburtine,
I was glad to get away to you,
my place on the edge of town,
and clear my chest of a bad cough
which my belly bestowed on me
for running after fancy dinners.

You see, since I was planning
to have dinner with Sestius,
I read over a speech of his
against Antius, the candidate—
full of poison and pestilence.
Immediately a bad chill
and frequent coughing shook me,
until I fled to your bosom
to cure myself with loafing
and a diet of nettles.

And now, recovered, I give you
my best thanks for not punishing
my mistake. And if I ever
again receive any of Sestius'
awful writings, I don't mind
if their icy chill produces
a terrible cold and coughing—
not in me but in Sestius,
who wouldn't invite me until
I'd read his nasty book.

45

Septimius, holding in his arms
his darling Acme, murmured:
"Acme, if I don't love you
to distraction—ready to go on
loving you every moment
through all the years to come
as completely and as desperately
as any lover can—
may I face a green-eyed lion
all alone, in Libya
or scorching India."

As he said this Love sneezed
in approval, on the left
and then on the right.

Then Acme, tilting her head
slightly backward and kissing
with her red mouth her darling's
love-drunken eyes, replied:
"Then Septimillius, my life,
we'll always serve the same master,
for an even fiercer fire
is burning inside of me."

As she said this, Love sneezed
in approval, on the left
and then on the right side.

And now, starting out with this
good omen, they love and are loved
with mutual affection.
Poor Septimius prefers
his Acme to all of Syria
and Britain. And faithful Acme
finds all her love and pleasure
in Septimius alone.
Who ever saw a happier couple
or a more auspicious love?

XLVI

IAM ver egelidos refert tepores,
iam caeli furor aequinoctialis
iucundis Zephyri silescit auris.
linquantur Phrygii, Catulle, campi
Nicaeaque ager uber aestuosae:
ad claras Asiae volemus urbes.
iam mens praetrepidans avet vagari,
iam laeti studio pedes vigescunt.
o dulces comitum valete coetus,
longe quos simul a domo profectos
diversae variae viae reportant.

46

Now spring brings back warm weather.
And now the gentle west winds
are silencing the fury
of the equinoctial gales.

Let's desert the Phrygian plains,
Catullus, and the fertile land
of burning Nicaea and fly
to the famous cities of Asia.

Now my mind is fluttering
in anticipation and yearns
to travel. Now my feet grow strong
with eagerness and joy.

Farewell, dear companions
who all started out together
from your distant homes and now
come back by many different ways.

47

Porcius and Socration—
Piso's two left hands—itching
with greed for the whole earth.
Has that circumcised Priapus
preferred you to my dear Veranius
and Fabullus? Are you attending
splendid, expensive banquets
in the middle of the day, while my friends
are walking the streets, looking
for invitations?

48

If I could kiss your honeyed eyes
as many times as I'd like,
Juventius, I'd kiss them
three hundred thousand times,
and even then I'd never
have enough—not if the harvest
of our kisses were thicker
than ripened grain.

49

Most eloquent of the descendants
of Romulus, Marcus Tullius—
of all who are and have been
and will be in years to come—
Catullus, the world's worst poet,
sends you his warmest thanks—
as much the worst of poets
as you are the best of lawyers.

50

Yesterday, Licinius,
having time on our hands, we played
for hours with my writing tablets,
since we didn't feel like doing
anything serious. We took turns
scribbling ridiculous verses
back and forth—in one meter
and then another—a dialog
accompanied by laughter and wine.

And then I came away
so worked up by your cleverness
and humor, Licinius,
that supper did me no good
and sleep refused to cover
my eyes with quietness.
Feverish and out of control
with excitement, I tossed all over
the bed, anxious for daylight—
to talk with you and be with you.

And afterward, when my body
lay on the bed half-dead—
worn out with the struggle—I made
this poem for you, dear friend,
from which you can see my suffering.

Now don't you dare be proud
or reject my prayers, I beg you,
dear fellow, or Nemesis
will give you the kind of punishment
you deserve. She's a powerful goddess.
Be careful you don't offend her.

51

He seems to me like a god,
or luckier than a god,
if that's possible, as he gazes
at you, sitting face to face,
and listens to your sweet laughter.

It takes away all my senses
and leaves me helpless, Lesbia,
when I look at you. Suddenly
there's no longer any voice
in my mouth.

My tongue is numb. A subtle
flame spreads through my body.
My ears ring with their own
sound, and both my eyes
are covered with night.

51a

Your trouble is laziness,
Catullus. You riot and rage
in unlimited laziness.
Laziness, before now,
has ruined kings and great cities.

52

Why is it, Catullus? Why
don't you hurry up and die?
Scabby Nonius sits
in a curule's chair, and Vatinius
backs up his lying promises
with a presumptive consulship.
Why is it, Catullus? Why
don't you hurry up and die?

53

I had to laugh at some fellow
in the crowd when my friend Calvus
described Vatinius's crimes
so marvellously. Lifting up
his hands in amazement, he cried
"Good heavens, what an eloquent midget."

54

Otto's head (it's very puny),
and farmerish Erius's
half-washed skin, and Libo's
delicate, lady-like farting—
I hope these things, if not everything
about them, will displease you,
Caesar, and also Fuficius,
that rejuvenated old lecher.
But now you'll be angry again
with my innocent iambics,
one and only general.

55

For heaven's sake, won't you tell me
where your hiding-places are?
I've been looking everywhere for you—
in the smaller Campus, in the Circus,
in every one of the bookstalls,
and in highest Jove's holy temple.

And I buttonholed all the tarts
that parade up and down in Pompey's
portico, and got nothing
but blank stares. Even so, my friend,
I kept asking for you: "Where's
my Camerius, you shameless girls?"

Then one of them, uncovering
her naked breasts, said "Look,
he's hiding in here, between
my rosy tits." Keeping up
with you these days, my friend,
is a labor of Hercules,
you keep yourself hidden so well.

Even if I were made of brass
like Talus, the guardian of Crete,
or as swift as Ladas or Perseus
with his winged feet, or were carried
on flying Pegasus or Rhesus'
fast pair of snow-white horses—
add to these all feather-footed
and winged things and summon
the winds' speed too, and harness
all these together, Camerius,
and bestow them on me, and I'd still
be exhausted to my marrow-bones
and worn out with endless fatigue,
searching for you, my friend.

Come, tell me where you're going
to be next. Out with it, bravely.
Speak up. Confess everything
in broad daylight. Is it
the milk-white girls who've got you
under their spell? If you keep
your tongue shut up in your mouth,
you'll throw away all the benefits
of love. Venus delights
in talking and tattling.

Well,
if you insist, go ahead—
keep your vocal cords locked up,
as long as you let *me* in on
the secret of your love affair.

56

Cato, this thing's so funny
and ridiculous you've got
to hear it and laugh at it.
Laugh, Cato, as heartily
as you love Catullus. The thing's
so funny and ridiculous.

I caught a young boy and girl
in the act, and immediately
(this should be pleasing to Dione)
fell on him with my stiff weapon.

57

They get along beautifully
together, those effeminate bastards,
crazy Mamurra and Caesar.
And no wonder. Like two filthy blotches,
one from Rome, the other from Formiae,
they're impressed upon one another
till they never can be washed out.

Like twins, sharing their diseases
and the same bed—both dabblers
in learning and literature,
one no more insatiable
than the other in stealing men's wives—
rivals and partners with the whores.

They get along beautifully
together, those effeminate bastards.

58

And now, Caelius, my Lesbia—
Lesbia herself—the Lesbia
Catullus loved more than himself
or anything he ever had—
is giving herself on street-corners
and in alleys to the descendants
of noble-minded Remus.

59

Rufa of Bologna,
the wife of Menenius,
plays dirty games with Rufulus.
She's the one you frequently see
in graveyards, stealing a supper
from the funeral pyre—chasing
the bread that comes rolling down
out of the fire, and lambasted
by the half-shaved body-burner.

60

Was it a lioness
from the mountains of Libya,
or Scylla with the barking heads
below the groin, that gave birth
to you, so fierce and hard
of mind that you hold in contempt
the voice of a suppliant
in his extremest need,
you savage-hearted one?

61

Urania's son—you who live
on Helicon's hill and carry
the delicate girl to the bridegroom—
o Hymenaeus Hymen,
o Hymen Hymenaeus,

bind your temples with blossoms
of sweet-smelling marjoram.
Put on the flame-colored veil
and come to us joyfully, wearing
yellow shoes on snow-white feet.

Summoned to this joyful day,
and carolling the wedding-songs
with a high-pitched, silvery voice,
beat the ground with your feet.
Shake the pine-torch in your hand.

Now Junia marries Manlius—
as lovely as Venus who lives
in Idalium when she stood
before Paris, the Phrygian judge—
a good girl bringing good omens.

Shining like the Asian myrtle
with its flowering branches
which the Hamadryad goddesses
nourish with dewy moisture
as a plaything for themselves.

Come this way, then. Take your leave
of the caves of Aonia
and the Thespian rocks, watered
from above by the cool streams
of the nymph Aganippe.

Call to her house the lady
full of desire for the bridegroom.
Bind her heart with love, as ivy,
clinging, spreading here and there,
twines itself around a tree.

Join with us, too, chaste virgins
for whom a similar day
is coming. Let's sing in tune:
"O Hymenaeus Hymen,
o Hymen Hymenaeus!"

That way the god may come
more willingly, hearing himself
summoned to his ritual—
minister of kindly Venus,
the coupler of honest love.

What god shall lovers who are loved
more properly call upon?
What god shall men worship more?
O Hymenaeus Hymen,
o   Hymen Hymenaeus!

The aged father invokes you
for his children. And young girls
loosen their girdles for you.
And for you the trembling bridegroom
listens with an eager ear.

You put the flowering bride,
taken from her mother's breast,
in the passionate bridegroom's arms,
o Hymenaeus Hymen,
o Hymen Hymenaeus!

Without you, Venus can't take
any pleasures which are approved
by opinion. But she can
if you're willing. What other god
dares match himself with this one?

No house can have its children
without you, and no father
count on progeny. But he can
if you're willing. What other god
dares match himself with this one?

A country which lacks your rites
can't produce guardians
for its borders. But it can
if you're willing. What other god
dares match himself with this one?

Unlock the locks on the doors!
The girl is coming. See the torches,
how they shake their golden hair!
....
....

....
....
Gentle shame makes her hesitate.
Yielding to it, she weeps the more
because she has to go on.

Stop crying, Aurunculeia.
You don't have to be afraid.
No woman more beautiful
will ever watch the bright day
coming up from the ocean.

A hyacinth stands like this
in the many-colored garden
of a rich landlord. The day
is going by while you linger.
Come forth, newly married girl.

Come forth, newly married girl,
and listen now, if you will,
to what we say. See the torches,
how they shake their golden hair!
Come forth, newly married girl.

Your husband will not choose
(lightly given to some wicked
adulteress and pursuing
shameful lusts) to sleep alone,
parted from your tender breasts,

but like the spiralling vine
that twines closely about a tree
will be twined in your embrace.
But the day is going by.
Come forth, newly married girl.

O bridal bed, which to all
....
....
....
.... by the bed's white foot.

What joys are coming for your lord
in the dimness of the night
or at noonday! What delight!
But the day is going by.
Come forth, newly married girl.

Lift up the torches, boys.
I see the bright veil coming.
Come sing together in tune:
"Hymen Hymenaeus, hail!
Hail Hymen Hymenaeus!"

Keep those naughty Fescennine jokes
silent no longer. Let the boy-love,
hearing his master's affection
is lost, not refuse to scatter
walnuts among the children.

Give nuts to the children, boy-love,
you pampered thing. You've played
with nuts long enough. You must serve
Talasius the marriage-god now.
Scatter the walnuts, boy-love.

Till the other day, boy-love,
you scorned the country wives
of the bailiffs. Now the barber
shaves your face, poor wretched creature.
Scatter the walnuts, boy-love.

They will say, sweet-smelling bridegroom,
you'll have trouble giving up
your boy-loves. Give them up, though.
Hymen Hymenaeus, hail.
Hail Hymen Hymenaeus.

We know the pleasures you've known
are permissible. But a husband
can't take the same liberties.
Hymen Hymenaeus, hail.
Hail Hymen Hymenaeus.

Bride, you be careful too.
Don't refuse what your husband wants
or he'll look for it somewhere else.
Hymen Hymenaeus, hail.
Hail Hymen Hymenaeus.

How rich and prosperous
this house your husband provides you.
It will serve you a long time—
(Hymen Hymenaeus, hail.
Hail Hymen Hymenaeus.)

—until white-haired old age,
nodding a trembling head,
says "yes" to all in all things.
Hymen Hymenaeus, hail.
Hail Hymen Hymenaeus.

Step with your golden feet
for luck across the threshold.
Enter the polished doorway.
Hymen Hymenaeus, hail.
Hail Hymen Hymenaeus.

See how, on the purple couch
inside, your husband, reclining,
concentrates his attention on you.
Hymen Hymenaeus, hail.
Hail Hymen Hymenaeus.

Inside his breast no less
than yours a passionate flame
is burning, but more secretly.
Hymen Hymenaeus, hail.
Hail Hymen Hymenaeus.

You boy in the purple-edged robe,
let go the girl's slender arm.
Let her come to her husband's bed.
Hymen Hymenaeus, hail.
Hail Hymen Hymenaeus.

You honest women, known
and trusted by aging husbands,
put the girl in the marriage-bed.
Hymen Hymenaeus, hail.
Hail Hymen Hymenaeus.

Now bridegroom, you may come.
Your wife's in the bridal-bed,
her face aglow with color
like white parthenike flowers
mingled with red poppies.

But god help me, husband,
you're no less handsome yourself.
Venus didn't overlook you.
But the day is going by.
Come, what are you waiting for?

You haven't waited very long.
Now you're coming. Gentle Venus
will help you, since you desire
what you desire openly
and don't hide your honest love.

Anyone who wants to count
your many thousand delights
must reckon the grains of sand
in Africa, first, or number
the incandescent stars.

Sport as you please, and soon
bear children. It isn't proper
that such an illustrious name
should go childless. May it rather
perpetuate itself forever.

May I see a little Torquatus,
reaching with his soft hands
from his mother's lap and smiling
sweetly up at his father
with tiny, half-open lips.

May he look like his father
Manlius, recognizable
easily, even by strangers,
and may his face proclaim
his mother's chastity.

May the good name of his mother
thus prove his inheritance,
like the matchless reputation
received by Telemachus
from his mother Penelope.

Come, virgins, close the doors.
We've amused ourselves long enough.
Live happily, happy pair.
Employ your vigorous youth
giving joy to one another.

62

BOYS

Evening has come, boys. Stand up.
Now at last the evening star
lifts his long-awaited light
into the sky. Now it's time
to leave the rich feasting and stand up.
Now the bride is coming. Now
let the wedding-song be sung.
　　　　O Hymen Hymenaeus,
　　　　come, Hymen Hymenaeus.

GIRLS

Look at the boys, unmarried girls.
Stand up to face them. For surely
the night-star's showing his fires
above Mount Oeta. Yes, it's true.
See how quickly they've jumped up.
It's not for nothing they've jumped up.
They'll sing something to surprise you.
　　　　O Hymen Hymenaeus,
　　　　come, Hymen Hymenaeus.

BOYS

Fellows, there's no easy victory
in store for us. See, the girls
are searching their memories
for what they've rehearsed. They haven't
rehearsed in vain. They'll come up
with something worth remembering.

And no wonder. They've concentrated
their whole mind upon it, while we
let our ears and our attention
wander in different directions.
We deserve to lose. Victory
favors hard work. Pay attention
now, at least. At any moment
they'll begin their singing. And we'll
be expected to answer them.
    O Hymen Hymenaeus,
    come, Hymen Hymenaeus.

GIRLS
Is there any crueller fire
burning in the sky than you,
Hesperus? You think nothing
of tearing a daughter from her mother's
embrace. You snatch the clinging girl
from her mother's arms and turn over
the chaste girl to a passionate
young man. Do even enemies
commit a greater cruelty
in a city when it's sacked?
    O Hymen Hymenaeus,
    come, Hymen Hymenaeus.

BOYS
Is there any happier fire
burning in the sky than you,
Hesperus? You seal with your flame
the marriage agreements which husbands
and fathers contracted beforehand
but never fulfil till your fires
have risen. What happier thing
can be granted by the gods
than this long-awaited hour?
    O Hymen Hymenaeus,
    come, Hymen Hymenaeus.

GIRLS

Friends, Hesperus has stolen
one of us.........................
....
....
....

BOYS

....
....
................for with your coming
the watchman is always vigilant.
Thieves hide themselves in the dark,
but many a time you catch them,
Hesperus, returning disguised
as the morning star. Unmarried girls
like to chide you with false complaints.
Pay no attention when they scorn
what their secret hearts desire.
      O Hymen Hymenaeus,
       come, Hymen Hymenaeus.

GIRLS

As a flower springs up, protected,
in a walled garden, concealed
from the herds, undisturbed by the plow—
winds caress it, the sun gives it strength,
showers nourish it. And many boys
and many girls cherish it.
But when the same flower is picked
with a sharp fingernail, and withers,
no boys and no girls covet it.

Just so a girl, while she remains
untouched, is loved by her friends.
But the moment her chaste flower
is lost, and her body defiled,
she's no longer attractive to boys
or popular with the girls.
   O Hymen Hymenaeus,
   come, Hymen Hymenaeus.

BOYS

As an unwedded vine grows up
in an empty field—it never
lifts itself up, and never
produces a full-blown grape.
Its slender body, bent down
by its own weight, twists along
the ground, and the highest branch
almost touches the root. No farmer
and no oxen cultivate it.
But if it happens to be mated
with a husband elm, many farmers
and many oxen tend it.
Just so an unmarried girl,
as long as she remains untouched,
grows old uncared for. But when
she's married, at the proper time,
to a suitable man, she'll be loved
even more by her husband, and be
less of a worry for her father.
Then don't refuse such a husband,
girl. It's not right to oppose
the man whom your father himself
has given you to—your own father
and mother, whom you ought to obey.

Your virginity isn't yours
alone. It's partly your parents'.
One third of it is your father's,
one third belongs to your mother,
and only a third is your own.
Don't oppose the two who've given
their shares to their son-in-law
together with your dowry.
       O Hymen Hymenaeus,
       come, Hymen Hymenaeus.

63

Carried across deep seas
in a fast ship, quick-footed Attis
entered the forests of Phrygia
and eagerly hurried to the dark
tree-circled place of the goddess.
And there, his mind bewildered,
driven by violent madness,
he castrated himself with a sharp stone.
Then, seeing his limbs deprived
of their manhood, and the fresh blood
still spotting the ground, *she* quickly
picked up a light tympanum
in her snow-white hands (the tympanum,
trumpet of your mysteries,
mother Cybele). And drumming
upon the hollow bull's hide
with delicate fingers, she began
singing to her companions
in a tremulous voice:

"Come, castrate priests, let's penetrate
the deep forests of Cybele
together. Let's go together,
a wandering herd of Our Lady
of Dindymus, eagerly seeking
exile in foreign places.
You've followed wherever I led you
as companions of the sect, enduring
wild waves and the bullying sea.
You've unmanned your bodies in violent
rejection of Venus. Now gladden
Our Lady's heart with swift wanderings.
Purge your minds of foolish delay.

Follow me, together, to Cybele's
Phrygian home—to the Phrygian forests
of the goddess, where clashing cymbals
sound, and tympanums reverberate,
and the Phrygian flute-player whistles
mournfully on his bending reed.
Where ivy-chapleted Maenads
toss their drunken heads and celebrate
their secret rites with piercing cries.
Where the goddess' worshippers hurry
ecstatically here and there.
That's the place we must hurry to
with our violent, quick dancing."

When Attis (the not-quite woman)
chanted this to her disciples,
the whole company yells aloud
suddenly, with quavering tongues.
The light tympanum drums again,
the curved cymbals clash again,
and the crowd moves quickly off
on hurrying feet toward green Ida.
And as Attis (raving, gasping
for breath, bewildered and uncertain
of her way) goes hurrying along
with her tympanum, leading the party
through the shadowy woods like a heifer
unbroken, shunning the yoke,
the castrate priests quickly follow
their hurrying leader. And when
they've come to Cybele's temple,
faint and tired from such exertions,
they fall asleep without their supper.
Lazy sleep covers up their eyes
with drooping oblivion,
and their delirious frenzy
leaves their minds to gentle rest.

But as soon as the gold-faced sun
looked out upon the white sky
with flashing eyes—and upon
the hard ground and the raging sea—
and scattered with his fresh hoof-beats
night's shadows, Sleep suddenly
abandoned Attis (awake now),
and goddess Pasithea welcomed him
to her fluttering breast. Then Attis,
her fanaticism quieted
after sleep, reviewed in her mind
what she had done, and clearly saw
what she had lost, and where it left her.
With seething heart she went running
back to the shore, and turning
eyes full of tears to the vast sea,
cried piteously to her homeland:

"Land that bore me, my native land,
which I left like a runaway slave
deserting his master, I've travelled
on foot to the forests of Ida
to live with snows and the frozen caves
of wild animals. In my frenzy
I go among their hiding-places.
Where, and in what direction,
shall I imagine you to be,
my homeland? My eyes want to turn
of their own accord and look out
toward you, as long as my mind
is free of its delirium
for a little while. Must I roam
forever in this wilderness,
far from home and separated
from country, possessions, friends,
and parents? Never to see
the forum again, or palaestra,
or stadium or gymnasium?

I'm doomed, poor miserable soul,
to complaining, forever and ever.
What human shape haven't I
experienced—a boy, a youth,
a young man, and now—a woman!
I, the flower of the gymnasium,
the pride of the wrestling-floor.
Friends crowded my doorway, warmed
my threshold, and decorated
my house with little garlands
of flowers whenever, at sunrise,
I used to leave my bed. But now
what am I—a priestess of the gods,
a votaress of Cybele,
a Maenad, only half myself,
a man without manhood! To live
in the snowy, frozen places
of green Ida. To live out my life
beneath the tall peaks of Phrygia
alone with the wild wood deer
and the forest-ranging boar.
Now indeed I grieve, and regret
the thing that I have done."

As soon as these words had issued
from her rosy lips (carrying
their surprising news to the ears
of the gods), Cybele, loosening
the yoke from her lions and goading
that fierce enemy of the herd
who pulled on the left, spoke thus:
"Come, violent beast," she said,
"go now and drive him this way
in his madness. Drive him back again
in a frenzy, to the forests—
that one who wants to be free
and escape from my sovereignty.

Come, lash your sides with your tail.
Whip yourself into a fury.
Make the whole place echo with roaring.
Shake your tawny mane savagely
on that brawny neck of yours."

Menacing Cybele said this
and loosened the yoke in her hand.
The beast, goading himself on,
stirs up a fury in his heart.
He runs and roars and breaks down
the bushes with his headlong charge.
And when he came to the edges
of the wave-whitened shore and spied
soft Attis beside the marble sea,
he springs. And Attis, terrified,
flees into the wildwood, to live there
all her life, a bondsmaid forever.

Goddess, great goddess Cybele,
great Lady of Dindymus, keep
your anger far from my house.
Goad others, mighty lady,
with your fury and your madness.

64

The pines which grew on Mount Pelion
in ancient times are reputed
to have swum through the wet sea-waves
to the Phasis' mouth and the land
of Aeetes, that time the chosen
young men (the pride of Greek manhood),
in hopes of stealing from Colchis
the fleece of gold, dared to venture
on the salt sea in a fast ship,
sweeping the dark-colored surface
with their firwood oars. Athena,
the goddess who guards the citadels
of our loftiest towns, made for them
with her own hands the sea-chariot
that flew before the wind's lightest breath,
fitting the pinewood planking
to the curved keel. That was the ship
which first acquainted Amphitrite,
the astonished sea-nymph, with voyaging.

As she plowed through the windy surface
with her prow, and the waves churned up
by the rowers turned white with foam,
wild faces rose from the frothy sea—
Nereids marvelling at the sight.
That day only, men saw with their eyes
the sea-nymphs exposing their bodies,
breasts naked, above the white sea.
Then Peleus, they say, burned with love
for Thetis. Then Thetis no longer
scorned marriage with a mortal.
Then Jupiter himself perceived
Peleus must marry Thetis.

Heroes born in that happy age—
hail to you, children of the gods!
Noble souls of noble mothers—
hail and hail again! I'll address you
frequently in my poem.
And you, blessed more than the others
by the marriage torches—Peleus,
bulwark of Thessaly, to whom
Jupiter himself (the father
of the gods himself) yielded up
his own darling! Didn't Thetis,
loveliest of all the Nereids,
embrace you, Peleus? Didn't Tethys
and Oceanus, who circles
the whole world with sea, permit you
to carry off their granddaughter?

And when, at the appointed time,
the long-awaited day had come,
all Thessaly gathered in the house.
The palace fills with a happy crowd
carrying presents before them,
their pleasure written on their faces.
Scyros is deserted. Everyone
has abondoned Tempe in Phthiotis
and Krannon's houses and the city
of Larissa, to meet at Pharsalus—
jamming the houses of Pharsalus.
No one tills the farms, and the necks
of young bullocks lose their calluses.
No curving hoes cultivate
the low-growing vines, and no ox
turns up clods with the sloping plowshare.
No pruner's hook thins the fruit trees.
Dirty rust fouls the lonely plows.

But Peleus' house (wherever
the rich palace stretches away)
is shining with silver and gold.
The chairs are ivory. Goblets
gleam on the tables. The whole place
is gay with bright royal treasure.
The marriage-bed of the goddess
is set in the middle of the house,
inlaid with polished ivory
and covered with a colored bedspread,
red and purple with sea-shell dyes.

The bedspread, embroidered with pictures
of legendary men, sets forth
the accomplishments of heroes
with marvellous skill. Ariadne
gazes from the wave-sounding shore
of Dia, watching Theseus
sailing away in his fast ship.
Violent passions fill her heart.
She still can't believe she's seeing
what she sees. And no wonder.
Just wakened from treacherous sleep,
she discovers she's been abandoned—
left helpless on the lonely shore.
But the fickle young man, deserting her,
is striking the sea with his oars,
casting his empty promises
to the unpredictable winds.

With troubled eyes, Minos' daughter
(like a Maenad carved from stone)
gazes after him, far off now
from the weedy shore, and great waves
of emotion rise in her heart.

No delicate headband binds up
her yellow hair. No flimsy veil
hides her naked breasts. No circling
breastband protects her milky nipples.
All these, fallen from her body,
the salt waves played with at her feet.
But she didn't care about the headband
or the floating veil. All her heart
and her mind and her troubled soul
were hanging on you, Theseus.
Miserable, beside herself
with constant grieving, and stung
with the pain Venus had planted
in her heart the moment Theseus
(boldly embarking from Piraeus'
curving shore) arrived at the Cretan
palace of the unjust king.

For they say that Athens, long ago,
forced by a terrible pestilence
to atone for the murdering
of Androgeos, used to send
its choicest young men and loveliest
unmarried girls for the feasting
of the Minotaur. And seeing
this curse afflicting his small city,
Theseus preferred to sacrifice
his own body for his dear Athens
rather than let such living corpses
be carried from Athens to Crete.
Driven by light winds in a fast ship,
he comes to confront proud Minos
and his magnificent palace.

The moment the girl looked at him
with love-struck eyes—the king's daughter,

whose sweet-smelling, virginal bed
still sheltered her like a mother's
soft embrace (lovely as the myrtles
that grow beside Eurotas River,
or the flowers of various colors
the breath of spring coaxes forth)—
she couldn't turn her burning look
away from him, till her whole body
caught the flame and she was on fire
to the center of her being.

Cruel boy-god of love, you stir up
such violent rages in the heart,
mixing joy with our suffering!
And you, too, goddess of Golgi
and leafy Idalium—what storms
you threw her burning heart into,
sighing for the yellow-haired stranger!
How many terrors she endured
in her fainting heart (how often
she turned paler than the gleam of gold)
as Theseus, eager to contend
with the savage monster, set out
to claim his reward of death or praise!
Silently she promised the gods
gifts to please them, and her prayers
weren't offered to them in vain.

Just as a hurricane tears up
an oaktree waving its branches
on Mount Taurus (or a pinetree
bearing cones and oozing resin),
wrenching loose the trunk with its blast—
uprooted, flung sideways, it topples
at full length, crushing everything
that gets in the way of its fall.
That's how Theseus battered down
that fierce creature—its great body

pinned to earth while the useless horns
gored the empty air. Then Theseus
retraced his steps, uninjured
and covered with glory—directing
his footsteps by the winding track
of the slender thread, lest the twisting
complexities of the labyrinth
prevent his escaping from the maze.

But why (digressing from the story
I began with) should I tell more?
How the girl, rejecting her father's
protection and her sister's embrace
(and even her mother's, who wept
for her miserable, lovesick child),
preferred Theseus' flattering love
to all these. Or how their ship
was driven to Dia's foaming shore.
Or how, when her eyes were sealed up
in gentle sleep, her false lover
abandoned her. Often, they say,
in the anguish of her burning mind,
she uttered a high-pitched wailing
from the depths of her heart, or climbed
desperately to the cliff-top
to strain her eyesight looking out
across the vast sea, or went running
to meet the incoming breakers
from the heaving sea—lifting up
her soft skirts to her naked thighs—
and cried out, with shuddering sobs
and tear-stained face, in her misery:

"So this is the reason you stole me
from my father's house, Theseus—
to leave me on this lonely shore!

Liar! Deceiver! So you're running
away in defiance of the gods—
carrying back home with you
your holy, broken promises!
Couldn't anything persuade you
to alter your cruel decision?
Wasn't there a spark of mercy
in your stony heart, to make you
take pity on me? This wasn't
the sort of thing you promised me
so persuasively once. You led me
to expect, instead of this misery,
a happy marriage—a happy life
together—vain hopes, blown away now
with the winds of heaven. After this,
let no woman listen to the vows
of any man, or hope any man's
words mean what they say. There's nothing
they'll hesitate to swear to—nothing
they won't promise in a moment,
when they've made up their lustful minds
to get hold of something they desire.
But as soon as they've satisfied
the desires of their greedy minds,
their words and their lies mean nothing
anymore. The truth is, I snatched you
from the middle of death's whirlpool—
preferring to lose my own brother
rather than fail you, my betrayer,
in the hour of your greatest need.
And for this I'll be left for the birds
and wild animals to dismember,
and lie here without a handful
of earth for my burial mound.

"What lioness bore you, under
a desert rock? What ocean
conceived you and spewed you forth
from its frothing waves—or was it
some Syrtis or rapacious Scylla
or vast Charybdis—who repay
the sweet gift of life in such fashion?
Even if you couldn't bring yourself
to marry me because you were afraid
of your father's authority
and old-fashioned strictness, you might
at least have taken me home with you
as a slave, to wait on you cheerfully
and lovingly—washing your white feet
with cool water, and covering
your bed with a purple bedspread.

"But why, beside myself with worry,
should I waste my breath crying out
to the ignorant air? It hasn't
any feeling and can't listen
to my questions or answer them.
Now he's almost halfway across
the sea and there's nobody else
to be seen on this desolate shore.
My bad luck continues to mock me
to the very end and denies me
even ears for my complaints.

"Almighty Jupiter, I wish
the Athenian ships had never
touched the shores of Crete in the first place,
or that deceitful voyager
(bringing his terrible offering
to the indomitable bull)
anchored his hawser on our island,
or that evil man (concealing
his cruel tricks with gentle looks)
rested in our palace as a guest!

Now where shall I turn? What comfort
can I cling to in my despair?
Shall I look toward the hills of Crete?
The violent, separating sea
divides us with its broad expanse.
Shall I hope for help from my father,
whom I left of my own accord
to follow a young man sprinkled
with my brother's blood? Or console myself
with the faithful love of a husband
who bends his strong oars against the sea,
running away? Here's a shore
without a house, and an island
without an inhabitant, hemmed in
by sea-waves, and no way to leave it.
No escape. No hope. Everything
around me is silent and desolate.
Everything speaks to me of death.
But my eyes won't close in death,
or the senses leave my weary body,
until I've demanded of the gods
a proper revenge for my betrayal
and invoked the heavenly ones'
protection in my final hour.

"Therefore, you avenging Furies,
who punish men's misbehavior
with the penalties they deserve
(your heads wreathed with serpent-hair
symbolize the anger exhaling
from your breasts)—come this way quickly
and hear the grievances which I,
poor wretched creature, must express
from my innermost being—helpless,
burning with anger, and blinded
with despair. Don't let my complaints
come to nothing, since they are spoken
from the bottom of my heart. Instead,

just as Theseus made up his mind
to desert me, make up your minds,
you goddesses, to destroy him
and everything that is his."

After she had poured out these words
from her troubled heart (demanding
revenge for his cruel behavior),
the ruler of the gods gave consent
by his potent nod. With that motion
the earth and the rough seas quaked,
and heaven shook its glittering stars.
But Theseus, blinding himself
with dark thoughts, let slip from his mind
all those injunctions he'd remembered
constantly till now, and failed
to hoist the glad signals to show
his worried father he'd sighted
the Athenian harbor safely.
For they say that when Aegeus
was entrusting his son to the winds
(earlier, as the ships were leaving
the city of the goddess), he embraced
the young man and gave these orders:

"My only son, dearer to me
than long life—just now restored to me
at the end of my old age—
my son, I'm forced to let you go
on this dangerous mission, since my fate
and your burning ambition tear you
away from me (against my will,
for my dimming eyes haven't yet
had enough of my dear son's face).
I won't send you off cheerfully
or with an easy heart, or permit you
to carry any signs of good fortune.
Instead I'll begin by uttering
many lamentations from my heart,

and dirty my white hair with handfuls
of ashes and dust, and finally
hang black sails from the swaying mast.
These dark Iberian canvases
will demonstrate my grief and my love.
But if she who lives in holy
Itonus (she who has promised
to protect our race and the city
of Erechtheus) is willing
you should stain your right hand with bull's blood,
then make sure these orders of mine
live stored up in your memory
where time can never erase them:
as soon as your eyes catch sight of
our hills, all the yardarms must lower
their funeral clothing, and the ropes
haul up white sails. When I see them
I'll know the good news and rejoice
that my luck has brought you home again."

At first Theseus kept these charges
constantly in mind. But later
they left him the way clouds leave
a snow-capped mountain's airy peak,
blown by the wind's breath. The father,
keeping watch from his palace-top,
wore his anxious eyes out with weeping.
And as soon as he saw the dark sails
he threw himself headlong from the cliff,
thinking Theseus had been destroyed
by a ruthless fate. Thus proud Theseus,
coming home to a house in mourning
for his father's death, experienced
for himself the kind of suffering
he'd inflicted on Minos' daughter
with his fickleness. While she,
gazing after the retreating ship
dejectedly, brooded over
all the sorrows in her wounded heart.

On another part of the bedspread
flower-fresh Bacchus is hurrying
along with his dancing Satyrs
and Nysan Silenuses—searching
for you, Ariadne—on fire
with love for you . . . . They raged madly
everywhere, yelling "Evoe!
Evoe!" and rolling their heads about
wildly. Some brandished thyrsuses
wreathed with vine-leaves. Others were tossing
the parts of a dismembered steer.
Some belted themselves with writhing snakes.
Some carried the dark mysteries
in closed boxes (the mysteries
non-initiates long vainly
to discover). Others beat tympanums
with their open palms or shook thin,
tinkling noises from brass cymbals.
Many carried horns which blared forth
their harsh blasts, and the barbarous pipe
screamed out its astonishing music.

Decorated with such handsome pictures,
the bedspread concealed the bed
enfolded in its drapery.
And after the young men of Thessaly
had examined it and satisfied
their eager curiosity,
they began to make room for the gods.
Then just as the west wind ruffles
the calm sea with its morning breath
and stirs up the jagged ripples
when dawn rises under the threshold
of the journeying sun—the wavelets
move slowly at first, urged along
by a gentle wind and echoing
with a gentle laughter. But later

they crowd closer as the wind rises
and sparkle in the purple light
as they move away. So the guests,
departing, left the palace courtyard
in every direction, going home.

After they had gone, Chiron came
first of the gods, from Mount Pelion,
bringing gifts from the woodland with him—
every kind of flower from the fields
and great mountains of Thessaly
and those that spring up by running streams
under the generating breath
of the warm west wind—mixed together
in rustic bouquets. And the house,
lightly touched with their pleasant odors,
was full of merriness and laughter.

Next came Peneus, from green Tempe,
girdled with its overhanging forests,
where the Thessalian women
and Doric girls dance together.
Not empty-handed, for he brings
lofty beechtrees, roots and all,
and straight-stemmed baytrees, and also
the waving planetree and the poplar
(supple sister of flame-struck Phaethon)
and tall cypresses. He planted them
all around the palace, close together,
so the courtyard would always be green
with a bordering of soft leaves.

Clever-minded Prometheus
followed after him, carrying
ancient scars from that punishment
suffered long ago when he hung
from a steep precipice—his arms
and legs chained to the solid rock.

Then came the father of the gods
with his holy wife and his sons,
leaving no one in heaven but you,
Phoebus, and your sister Diana,
who lives in the mountains of Idrus.
For she scorned Peleus, as you did,
and preferred not to be present
for Thetis' marriage celebration.

After they had seated themselves
on the ivory chairs, the tables
were piled high with food of all kinds,
while the Parcae (their bodies shaking
with a palsied motion) began
chanting their prophetic verses.
White robes wrapped their trembling bodies,
bordered with red at the ankles,
and their white hair was decorated
with red ribbons. With busy hands
they performed their eternal ritual.
Their left hand held the distaff,
covered with soft wool, while the right one
(fingers turned up) deftly drew out
the threads and shaped them and then
(fingers downward) twirled the spindle
quickly and smoothly, while their teeth
bit at the yarn continually
to make the work even. Particles
of wool bitten off where they stood out
from the central thread were clinging
to their thin, dry lips. At their feet
wicker baskets held the fleeces
of white wool. Then with high-pitched voices
they chanted (still plucking the fleeces)
fatal prophecies in godlike song—
songs no aftertime shall prove untrue:

"Peleus, pride of Thessaly,
Jupiter's darling (adding luster
to a distinguished lineage
with great deeds)—receive these oracles,
truly spoken, which the Sisters
reveal to you this joyful day.
And you, on whom the fates depend,
run, spindles, spinning the woof-threads.

"Now Hesperus will soon appear,
bringing you what bridegrooms long for,
and underneath that fortunate star
your bride will come to you, flooding
your heart with soul-disturbing love—
lying with you in lazy sleep,
her smooth arm under your strong neck.
Run, spindles, spinning the woof-threads.

"No house ever brought together
such lovers beneath one roof before.
No love ever before joined lovers
in such harmony as this
between Thetis and Peleus.
Run, spindles, spinning the woof-threads.

"A son shall be born to you
unacquainted with fear—Achilles,
known to his enemies only
for his broad chest, never for his back—
frequent winner in the long race,
who'll outrun the swift, flame-footed deer.
Run, spindles, spinning the woof-threads.

"No hero shall compare with him
in war when the Phrygian rivers
flow with Trojan blood and Agamemnon
levels Troy's walls after long fighting.
Run, spindles, spinning the woof-threads.

"Mothers at their sons' funerals
shall often be forced to acknowledge
his terrible strength and mighty deeds
as they let down their tangled hair
(whitened with ashes) and batter
their withered breasts with feeble hands.
Run, spindles, spinning the woof-threads.

"For like a reaper mowing down
yellow fields beneath a hot sun,
he'll strike down the Trojan bodies
with his devastating sword.
Run, spindles, spinning the woof-threads.

"Scamander River, as she pours
her swift current into the Hellespont,
shall bear witness to his great valor
when he chokes her bed with corpses
and makes her run warm, mixed with blood.
Run, spindles, spinning the woof-threads.

"And the prize awarded him in death
shall bear witness, when the pyre,
heaped high on his funeral mound,
holds a slaughtered girl's white body.
Run, spindles, spinning the woof-threads.

"For as soon as the fates permit
the weary Greeks to break the chain
forged round the Dardanian city
by Neptune, his tomb shall be watered
with Polyxena's blood, as she falls
under the two-edged sword
like a sacrificial victim—
slumping forward where she's kneeling
a decapitated corpse.
Run, spindles, spinning the woof-threads.

"Come, then, consummate the love
your souls long for. Let the bridegroom
receive the goddess in marriage
joyfully. And let the bride
be given immediately
to the impatient bridegroom.
Run, spindles, spinning the woof-threads.

"When her nurse visits her again
at daybreak, she won't be able
to circle her neck with the ribbon
she wore yesterday. And her mother
needn't worry about her daughter
sleeping by herself in a quarrel
or give up hoping for grandchildren.
Run, spindles, spinning the woof-threads."

The Parcae sang these songs, long ago,
foretelling Peleus' happiness
from their knowledge of things to come.
For the gods, in those ancient days
before religion was neglected,
used to visit the pious homes
of heroes in their bodily shapes
and show themselves before gatherings
of men. And often the father
of the gods himself, revisiting
his shining temple when the yearly
celebrations came round, would see
a hundred bulls fall to the ground
on holy days. Often Dionysus,
roaming the summit of Parnassus,
drove his screaming Thyades along
with their streaming hair, and citizens
of Delphi rushed forth eagerly
from all parts of the town to welcome him,
graciously, with smoking altars.

And often, in the deadly conflict
of war, Mars and swift Minerva
or the virgin Nemesis in person
exhorted armed bodies of men.

But after the earth was corrupted
with unspeakable crimes and all men
banished honor from their lustful souls,
and brothers sprinkled their hands
with brothers' blood, and a son
forgot to mourn his dead parents,
and a father longed for the death
of his own young son (to be free
to deflower a young virgin
as his second wife), and a mother
without shame (shamelessly coupling
with her own unknowing son)
wasn't afraid of offending
the household gods—after these things,
right and wrong are everywhere confounded
in madness and crime, and the gods'
righteous will is turned away from us.
They're no longer willing to visit
with companies of men or permit
the bright daylight to shine on them.

65

Hortalus, I'm exhausted
with continual grieving. And sorrow
distracts me from those learned virgins,
the Muses, whose lovely conceptions
my mind's too upset by trouble
to be able to utter anymore.
For a creeping wave from Lethe River
has recently washed the pale foot
of my brother (snatched from our sight),
on whom Trojan earth lies heavy
under the shore of Rhoeteum.

Brother, I loved you better
than my own life. Now I'll never
talk with you again, or listen
while you tell me what you've been doing.
I'll never set eyes on you again.
But I won't stop loving you
and singing lonely songs about your death—
like the Daulian nightingale,
singing in the thick boughs' shade
and weeping for Itylus.

But in spite of all my sadness
I'm sending these verses, Hortalus,
translated from Callimachus,
so you won't think your request for them
was blown away by the breezes
or slipped my mind, like the apple
(a secret gift from her lover)

that falls from an innocent girl's
chaste lap. Poor thing, she's forgotten
about it (hidden in the folds
of her dress) until she jumps up
when her mother comes, and it tumbles
out. Then down and away
it goes rolling, while a blush
creeps self-consciously over
the girl's embarrassed face.

66

Conon, the famous astronomer,
studied all the constellations
and discovered the risings and settings
of the stars (how the bright fire
of the hurrying sun disappears—
how the stars withdraw at certain times—
how sweet love calls Diana away
from the heavenly circuit and holds her
secretly in Patmos' cave).
That same Conon saw me shining
bright and clear among heaven's lights—
a lock of Berenice's hair
she promised to many goddesses
(stretching out her smooth white arms
in supplication) when her king,
newly married—still showing signs
of the sweet night-battle he'd fought
for her virgin maidenhead—went off
to lay waste the Syrian border.

Is Venus really hated by brides?
Or are they false, those complainings
they pour out so abundantly
in their bedrooms, causing their parents
so much worry? I swear by the gods,
their protests are lies! My queen
taught me that with all her weeping
the time her new husband went away
to that awful war. I suppose
you'll say it wasn't the loneliness
of an empty bed that made you cry
but the sad parting from your brother
that was eating your heart out with sorrow!
Then worry snatched away your senses
altogether, and you fainted.
And yet I remember very well

how brave you've always been, from the time
you were a little girl. Remember
the bold action by which you attained
a royal marriage—something
an even braver person mightn't
have had the courage for? And yet,
on that unhappy occasion
when you sent your husband away,
what words you uttered! Jupiter!
How often you rubbed at your eyes
with your hand! What kind of a god
brought about such a change in you?
Or is it that lovers can't stand
being separated very long
from the person they love? And then
you pledged me, with the blood of bulls,
to all the gods for your dear husband,
if he came back successfully.
Soon he added captive Asia
to the territories of Egypt,
and that's why I'm now fulfilling
your original offer of a gift—
delivered as promised to the gods.

I was cut off against my will
from your head, o Queen. Against my will,
I swear, by you and by your head
(and may anyone who swears falsely
by these suffer just punishment).
But who can claim to be a match
against steel? Even a mountain
was cut down (the largest anywhere
in all places the shining sun
travels over) that time the Medes
built a new sea and barbarian
youths sailed their ships through the middle
of Mount Athos. What can hair do
when things like this succumb to steel?
O Jupiter, let the whole race

of Chalybes perish, and whoever
first began searching underground
for veins and forging hard iron!

My sister locks (separated
from me just before) were bewailing
my fate, when Egyptian Memnon's
brother Zephyr (the winged horse
of Locrian Arsinoe)
appeared, striking the air
with beating wings. Lifting me up,
he flew off through the shadowy air
and placed me in Venus' chaste lap.
The Lady of Zephyrium
herself (a Greek inhabitant
of Egypt's shore) had sent her servant
for the purpose, so that the crown
of gold from Ariadne's head
wouldn't be set up all alone
among the varied lights of the sky,
but I, the consecrated spoil
from Berenice's yellow head,
might shine there too. Wet with spray,
and carried to the dwelling-place
of the gods, I was established there
as a brand new constellation
among the ancient ones. Nearest
the stars of Virgo and fierce Leo,
and close to Lycaon's daughter,
Callisto, I wheel toward my setting
well ahead of slow Boötes,
who immerses himself very late
in deep Ocean. But though the footsteps
of the gods press close upon me
at night, and by day I'm restored
to white-headed Tethys herself
(with your permission let me say this,
virgin Nemesis, for I won't hide
the truth because of any fear—

even if the stars should pull me
to pieces with their angry words,
I won't hold back from uttering
the feelings locked up in my heart)—
instead of rejoicing in these things,
I'm tortured by the realization
that I'm separated forever
from the head of my mistress, with whom,
while she was a virgin, I drank
many thousands of the perfumes
I'm cut off from now altogether.

Now you whom the marriage torches
bring together with their welcome light,
don't yield your bodies to your husbands,
however eager, or throw open
your robes to your naked nipples,
till you've poured from the onyx jar
a suitable libation for me—
but only if you've respected
the marriage laws in a chaste bed.
As for her who has given herself
in unlawful adultery—
let the worthless dust drink up
her false, ineffectual gift.
For I want no gifts from anyone
who's unworthy. Rather, you brides,
may harmony and lasting love
live forever in your houses.

And you, my Queen, when you're gazing
at the stars and worshipping Venus
on festival days, don't let me
(since I'm yours) go unprovided
with perfumes, but offer me instead
many gifts. O, why must the stars
hold me here? If only I could be
a royal lock of hair again.
I wouldn't care if Orion
shone next door to Aquarius!

67

CATULLUS

Greetings, house-door, loved by a gentle
husband and also by his father—
may Jupiter add to your blessings.
They say you served Balbus well
in the days when the old man himself
owned this house. On the other hand,
you serve his son rather badly,
they say, ever since the old man
was laid out and a married woman
rules the roost. Tell me about it.
Why are you accused of fickleness
and abandoning your loyalty
of long standing to the master?

DOOR

As I hope to please Caecilius,
to whom I belong, it isn't
my fault, though everyone says it is,
and no one can point to any crime
I've committed. Of course, people try
to blame everything on the door,
and whenever some misbehavior
comes to light, everybody shouts
"Door, it's all your fault!" at me.

CATULLUS

It isn't enough to deny it
on your say-so alone. Prove it
in such a way that anyone
will see it and be convinced of it.

DOOR

How can I? Nobody asks me
or makes any effort to find out.

CATULLUS

I do. Don't hesitate to tell me.

DOOR

In the first place, then, it isn't true
that she was delivered to us
a virgin. Not that her husband
slept with her ahead of time.
He couldn't get that lazy tool,
hanging limp as a tender beet,
halfway out of his underclothing.
They say it was his own father
who violated the son's bed
and brought shame to this unlucky house—
whether his incestuous soul
was on fire with a blinding passion
or his lackadaisical son
was impotent, and more vigorous
means had to be found elsewhere
for taking the girl's maidenhead.

CATULLUS

That's an edifying example
of paternal consideration
you're telling me about. A father
cuckoldizing his own son!

DOOR

And yet that isn't the only thing
Brixia claims to know about—
Brixia town, lying under
Chinea's fortress, through which
yellow Melos' gentle waters run—

Brixia, dear mother-city
of my Verona. She tells tales
of affairs with Postumius
and Cornelius, with both of whom
she was guilty of adultery.

CATULLUS

At this point someone will ask
"How do you know all this, house-door?
You never have a chance to leave
your master's threshold or hear
people gossiping, but stay fixed
to this doorpost with nothing to do
but open the house and close it."

DOOR

I've frequently heard her talking
secretly, alone with her maids,
about these wicked deeds of hers,
mentioning the ones I spoke of
by name (supposing, I imagine,
that I'd neither an ear nor a tongue).
And she added another one
besides, whom I'd rather not mention
by name, lest he lift his red eyebrows.
He's a tall man who was involved
at one time in a famous lawsuit—
a case of false pregnancy
and a trumped-up paternity charge.

68

Oppressed by bitter calamities
and misfortune, you've sent me this letter
written in tears and imploring me
to come to the help of a shipwrecked man
cast up by the sea's frothing waves,
and rescue him from death's doorway,
since holy Venus won't permit him
to find rest in sweet sleep (all alone
in his widowed bed) or the Muses
beguile him with the lovely songs
of the ancient poets while his mind
is sleepless with anxiety.
This is gratifying to me,
since you consider me your friend
and apply to me for the favors
of the Muses and of Venus.

But so that my own difficulties
won't be unknown to you, Manius,
and you won't think I'm neglecting
the obligations of a friend,
listen to what waves of bad luck
I'm immersed in too, and don't ask
for gifts that a happy man might give
from an unfortunate like me.

At that time when the white toga
had just been conferred upon me—
when my first-flowering manhood
was still in its merry springtime—
I played games enough. The goddess
who mixes bitter and sweetness
with love's cares isn't unknown to me.
But my brother's death has swept away
all my interest in such matters.

O my brother, taken away
to leave me suffering. Brother,
your death has shattered my happiness.
With you our whole house is buried.
With you my one and only joy
lies dead (your sweet love nourished it
while you were alive). With your death
I've banished from my mind entirely
all delight in poetry and love.

Therefore, when you write "Your being
in Verona, Catullus, brings shame
upon you, since everybody
who is anybody in Rome
is warming his frozen members
in your bed while you're away from it"—
it's all a bit sad, Manius,
but not much of a disgrace.
And so I know you'll forgive me
for not sending you as a gift
something grief has taken away from me
and made me incapable of.

The reason I haven't many copies
of my poems with me is this:
I live in Rome. It's my house,
my home. It's where I spend my time.
Only one box out of many
follows me here. That's how it is,
and I wouldn't want you to suppose
it's because of unwillingness
or boorishness that you haven't
been supplied with everything you asked for.
I'd have offered without your asking
if I'd had anything to give.

68a

Goddesses, I can't help telling you
about the affair that Allius
helped me in (and how very helpful
his efforts were)—lest hurrying,
obliterating time hide his deeds
in oblivion. I'll tell you,
hoping you'll tell many thousands
and let this paper go on speaking
even after it grows old . . . . Let him
become increasingly famous
in death, and don't let any spider
(weaving her flimsy web in air)
perform her work over Allius'
neglected reputation. You know
already the kind of trouble
that double-dealing goddess, Venus,
made for me, and the occasion
on which she gave me a scorching—
that time I was boiling like Mount Aetna
or the hot springs of Thermopylae
(between Oeta and the Gulf
of Malia). My troubled eyes
never stopped wearing themselves out
with continual weeping, and my cheeks
were streaming with unhappy tears.

The way a rivulet leaps forth,
clear as light, from the mossy rocks
on the windy peak of a mountain,
and after it goes tumbling headlong
down the steep mountainside, passes
right through the middle of a crowd
of people—a sweet refreshment
for the sweating traveller, when
oppressive heat cracks the parched soil.

Or the way sailors, tossed about
by a black tempest, are visited
afterward by a more gentle,
favorable breeze they had prayed for
first to Pollux and then to Castor—
such a comfort to me was Allius.

He opened a broad path for me
across a closed field. He gave me
and my lady a house—a place
where we could exercise our love
together. There my white goddess
directed her gentle step and paused
on the smooth doorsill, pressing it
with her shining foot and trim sandal,
just as Laodamia came,
long ago, on fire with love,
to Protesilaus' house (begun
in vain, since no victim's holy blood
had first pacified the lords of heaven).
May I never long for anything
so eagerly, virgin Nemesis,
that I presume to undertake it
without the blessing of the gods!

How much the thirsty altar
craves the blood of sacrifices
Laodamia learned from the loss
of her husband—forced to let go
her arms from the neck of her bridegroom
before the coming of one winter
and then another had satisfied
their greedy love with its long nights,
preparing her to survive
the breaking-up of their marriage,
which the Fates knew wasn't far off
if he went as a fighter to Troy.

For at that time Troy had begun
to stir up the leaders of the Greeks
against itself with Helen's rape.
Cursed Troy, the common sepulcher
of Europe and Asia—Troy,
the bitter grave of noble men
and noble deeds—it was you
that inflicted miserable death
on my brother. O brother, taken
from me in my sorrow. Brother,
light of my happiness, taken
away, to leave me suffering.
With you our whole house is buried.
With you my one and only joy
lies dead (your sweet love nourished it
while you were alive). A strange land
holds you now in its distant soil,
far away—not among familiar
graves or entombed near the ashes
of your family, but buried
in sinister, unlucky Troy.

At that time, they say, all the young men
of Greece hurried there together,
deserting the fireplaces
in their homes, to prevent Paris
from passing his time quietly
in a peaceful bed, enjoying
his stolen mistress without challenge.

That's how it happened that you,
loveliest Laodamia,
lost a husband sweeter than life
and soul to you. The tides of love
had engulfed you in a whirlpool
and plunged you in a deep abyss—
as deep, according to the Greeks,
as the gulf near Cyllenian
Pheneus which drains the marshes

(drying out the fertile cropland)
and which the falsely-fathered son
of Amphitryon is reputed
to have dug long ago by cutting
out a mountain's center, that time
he killed the Stymphalian monsters
with his never-swerving arrows
on orders from a meaner lord—
so that the doorway of heaven
might be entered by one more god
and Hebe shouldn't long remain
a virgin. But deeper than that gulf
was your deep love, which taught you,
though unbroken, to bear the yoke.

Not so dear to an old grandfather
is the head of the late-born child,
nursed by his only daughter,
who shows up at the last moment
as heir to the family fortune,
and when his name is written down
in a will before witnesses,
puts an end to the unnatural
hopes of a baffled relative
(frightening that vulture away
from the grandfather's hoary head).
No she-dove ever delighted
so fully in her snow-white mate,
though they say she snatches kisses
and bites and bills more wantonly
than the most insatiable woman.
You alone surpassed the great passion
of these, when once you were united
in love with your yellow-haired husband.

Deigning to yield to her in this
little or not at all was she,
the light of my life, when she came
into my arms, and around her
bright Cupid fluttered here and there,
shining in his yellow tunic.
And though she isn't contented
with Catullus alone, I'll put up
with the rare infidelities
of my discreet lady, rather
than make a nuisance of myself
the way fools do. Often Juno
herself, the queen of the goddesses,
swallowed her anger at her husband's
amorous misdeeds, having learned
of the many secret love affairs
of insatiable Jove. And though
it isn't proper for mortals
to compare themselves with the gods,
may I similarly rid myself
of the unrewarding burden
of behaving like a worried parent.
After all, she didn't come to me
on her father's arm, to a house
smelling of Syrian perfumes,
but gave me, in the silent night,
secret gifts, stolen from the bosom
of her husband himself. Therefore
it's enough if she reserves for me
that day she marks with a whiter stone.

This gift of verses, Allius,
the best I was capable of,
I send you in repayment
for many favors, so this day
and that day, one after another,

won't tarnish your reputation
with foul rust. May the gods add to it
all those many gifts which Themis
used to bestow on pious men
in the old days. May you be happy,
both you and she who is your life,
and that house in which my lady
and I were happy together,
and he who first made us acquainted
(from whom all these good things were born
for me), and above all by far
she who's dearer to me than myself—
my bright one, whose life alone
makes it good for me to be alive.

69

Rufus, you needn't be surprised
that no woman wants to submit
her tender thighs to your embrace—
not even if you soften her up
with gifts of expensive dresses
or a lovely jewel, clear as light.

What's ruining your reputation
is the ugly rumor they're spreading
that you've got a stinking goat
under your armpits. They're all
afraid of it. And no wonder.
It's a damned unpleasant animal
for a pretty girl to go to bed with.

So kill off that terrible threat
to their noses, or stop wondering
why they're running away from you.

70

My woman says there's no one
she'd rather be married to than me—
not even if Jupiter himself
laid siege to her. So she says—
but anything a woman tells
an eager lover should be written
on the wind and running water.

71

If ever a poor fellow
was afflicted with an unholy
stinking under the armpits
or suffered for his transgressions
from a gout that crippled him up,
that rival or yours who keeps
your girl friend busy in bed
has contracted both maladies
in marvellous fashion. And so,
whenever he's doing it with her,
you're revenged on both of them.
She's overcome with the stink
and the gout's half killing him.

LXXII

DICEBAS quondam solum te nosse Catullum,
Lesbia, nec prae me velle tenere Iovem.
dilexi tum te non tantum ut vulgus amicam,
sed pater ut gnatos diligit et generos.
nunc te cognovi: quare etsi impensius uror,
multo mi tamen es vilior et levior.
qui potis est? inquis. quod amantem iniuria talis
cogit amare magis, sed bene velle minus.

72

Lesbia, you used to tell me
nobody really understood you
except Catullus, and you wouldn't
take Jove in preference to me.

In those days I loved you
not just like an ordinary fellow
and his girl, but the way a father
loves his sons and sons-in-law.

I know all about you now,
and although I'm more violently
in love than ever, I find you
a lot cheaper and more frivolous.

You wonder how that can be?
It's because a trick like this
makes a lover love you all the more
but like you a good deal less.

73

Stop hoping to deserve any thanks
from anyone at all, or expecting
anyone can ever be capable
of gratitude. All the world's
ungrateful. Doing a kindness
counts for nothing. It's a bore,
and worse than a bore. That's how
it works out for me, since no one
shows such bitterness and hostility
as that fellow who used to consider me
his one and only friend.

74

Gellius had heard that his uncle
had the habit of raising hell
if anyone went in for adultery
or even talked about such things.

He wasn't going to let that
happen to him. So he seduced
his uncle's own wife, and now uncle's
as silent as Harpocrates.

He did exactly as he pleased
after that. And the way things stand,
he could take on uncle himself
and uncle wouldn't say a word.

75

My spirit has been brought so low
by your faithlessness, Lesbia,
and has worked such ruin on itself
by its own devotion, that now
it can never think kindly of you,
even if you should become
the best of women. Or stop loving you,
no matter what you do.

76

If there's any pleasure for a man
in remembering the favors
he's done in the past and knowing
he's been a true friend, who never
broke a sacred trust or swore falsely
by the gods to deceive other men
in any agreement, there are still
many satisfactions, Catullus,
remaining from that thankless love
of yours, in the long years ahead.

For whatever kindnesses men
can promise or carry out
for one another have been promised
and carried out by you. All this
has been wasted on an ungrateful
soul, but why torment yourself
any longer? Why not harden
your heart and forget all that
and stop making yourself unhappy—
flying in the face of the gods?

It's hard to give up suddenly
a friendship of long standing.
It's hard, but you've got to do it
somehow. It's your only hope—
your one way out. You must do it,
whether it's possible or not.

You gods, if you're merciful,
or if you ever brought relief
to someone on the verge of death,
take notice of me in my suffering,
and if I've led a decent life,
take away from me this plague
and destruction which is creeping
into my innermost being
and driving out happiness
altogether from my heart.

I won't ask any longer
that she love me in return
or develop a sense of shame,
because that's impossible.
I want to be stronger myself
and get rid of this morbid sickness.
Gods, grant me this for my piety!

77

Rufus, I trusted you
as a friend—mistakenly
and all for nothing. (For nothing,
did I say? Rather, it cost me
plenty of misery.) Is this
how you wormed your way into me,
burned through my guts, and tore
away all my happiness?
Tore it away, damn you—
bitter poison of my existence—
you cancerous growth on my friendship!

78

Gallus has two brothers.
One has a very pretty wife,
the other a charming son.

Gallus is most obliging.
He panders beautifully.
So he puts the pretty boy
in bed with the lovely lady.

Gallus is a fool. Can't he see
(while he's teaching the art of seducing
an uncle's wife) that he's an uncle
who's got a wife of his own?

78a

What's bothering me is this,
that you've mixed up your filthy spit
with a pure girl's pure kisses.
But you won't get away with it
scot free. All the generations
will know you, and old lady Rumor
will tell them what you were.

79

Lesbius is a pretty boy.
And why not, since Lesbia
prefers him to you, Catullus,
and your whole family.

But this pretty boy would sell
Catullus and all his tribe
for three friendly kisses
from any bigshot in town.

80

Tell me, Gellius, why is it
that those rosy lips of yours
are whiter than the winter snow
when you leave home in the morning
or when you finally get up
in the middle of the afternoon,
after a quiet siesta?

There's something funny going on,
for sure. But is it true—
what the gossips are whispering—
that you're a pervert? It's true,
all right. Poor little Victor
looks all worn out, and your lips
tell us what you've been up to.

81

Juventius, wasn't there anyone
in this whole city (some decent
fellow you might suddenly
take a liking to) except him—
that stranger of yours from somewhere
near plague-infested Pisaurum?
He's as yellow as a gilded statue—
that one who's your favorite now
(the one you have the audacity
to prefer to me). Don't you see
what a stupid thing you're doing?

82

Quintius, if you want Catullus
to owe you his eyes, or anything
(if there is anything) more precious
than his eyes, don't take away
the thing he loves more than his eyes
or whatever there is more precious
than his eyes.

83

Lesbia runs me down
in front of her husband. The fool
is delighted with that. Stupid ass,
you don't understand these things.
If she hadn't even mentioned me
because she'd forgot, she'd be
all right. But the way she scolds
and carries on means not only
she remembers, but more important,
it's got her upset. In other words,
she loves me, so she talks.

LXXXIV

CHOMMODA dicebat, si quando commoda vellet
  dicere, et insidias Arrius hinsidias,
et tum mirifice sperabat se esse locutum,
  cum quantum poterat dixerat hinsidias,
credo, sic mater, sic Liber avunculus eius,
  sic maternus avus dixerat atque avia.
hoc misso in Syriam requierant omnibus aures:
  audibant eadem haec leniter et leviter,
nec sibi postilla metuebant talia verba,
  cum subito affertur nuntius horribilis,
Ionios fluctus, postquam illuc Arrius isset,
  iam non Ionios esse, sed Hionios.

84

When Arrus wanted to say "commoda"
it would come out "chommoda".
And "insidias" turned into
"hinsidias". He was sure
he was speaking remarkably well
whenever he said "hinsidias"
at the top of his voice. I suppose
that's the way his mother said it,
and Uncle Liber, and his grandfather
and grandmother on the mother's side.

When he was sent into Syria
all our ears had a holiday.
They heard the same words pronounced
smoothly and gently. After that
they lost their fear of such words,
till suddenly the shocking news
arrived that the Ionian
Sea wasn't "Ionian"
anymore. Since Arrius
showed up there, it's "Hionian".

85

I hate and I love.
Why do I do it, you ask,
perhaps, and I can't tell you.
But I know it's true, and it hurts.

86

For many, Quintia's a beauty.
To me, she's tall, well-built,
and she has a nice complexion.
I'll admit her good points and still
deny that she's a real beauty.
Somehow there's no sparkle,
no spice in that magnificient body.
It's Lesbia that's beautiful.
In looks, she has everything,
and she's stolen all the sex appeal
from all the others for herself.

87

No other woman can say,
honestly, that she's been loved
as much as you've been loved
by me, my Lesbia.
There was never such faithfulness
in any relation as I've
discovered in my love for you.

88

What's he up to now, that Gellius,
keeping these scandalous vigils
all night long and stark naked
with his own mother and sister?
And what does he mean, preventing
his uncle from playing the husband?
Has he any idea how much sin
he's guilty of, that Gellius?
So much that far-off Tethys
and Oceanus, the father
of the sea-nymphs, couldn't wash it
away. For there isn't any crime
left for him to aspire to—
not even if he managed
to practice incest with himself.

89

Gellius is thin. And why not?
With such an indulgent mother
and a charming sister, so buxom
and lively, and an obliging
uncle, and female cousins
all over the place—
how can he help being skinny?
Even if he never touched anything
except what he never ought to touch,
it's easy to see why he's so skinny.

90

From this unholy union
between Gellius and his mother
a "magus" might be born
and acquire the art of soothsaying.

For if there's any truth
in the Persians' outlandish religion,
a magus must be begotten
by a mother and her own son.

So perhaps their offspring can worship
the gods with appropriate songs
while melting the sacrificial fat
in the altar flame.

91

It wasn't because I supposed
you were really honorable
or able to restrain yourself
from any sort of vice, Gellius,
that I hoped you'd be honest with me
in my desperate, unhappy
love affair. It was because
I saw that the one for whom
I was burning with such a passion
wasn't your mother or your sister.
And although we'd been acquainted
a long time, I didn't think that
was enough to tempt you. You thought
it was enough. You always
prefer those vices in which
some kind of dirtiness is mixed.

92

Lesbia always runs me down.
She never stops talking about me.
I'm damned if she doesn't love me.
How can I tell? Because
it's exactly the same with me.
I'm always running her down,
but I'm damned if I don't love her.

93

I haven't the slightest interest
in trying to please you, Caesar.
It makes no difference to me
whether you're white or black.

94

Mentula's a fornicator,
you say? That's true enough.
Mentula's a fornicator.
But that's about like saying
birds fly, fish swim.

95

My friend Cinna's *Smyrna*
is published at last—
nine summers and winters
after it was begun.
Meanwhile Hortensius
has brought out five hundred thousand
verses in one.

The *Smyrna* will be circulated
as far away as the deep-
channeled river Satrachus,
and the centuries will grow old
and gray, reading the *Smyrna,*
while Volusius's *Annals*
will die right there beside
the Padua and provide
loose sheets for wrapping mackerel.

Let me cherish the modest verses
of my friend, while the mob raves
about their long-winded Antimachus.

XCVI

SI quicquam mutis gratum acceptumve sepulcris
*   accidere a nostro, Calve, dolore potest,*
quo desiderio veteres renovamus amores
*   atque olim amissas flemus amicitias,*
certe non tanto mors immatura dolori est
*   Quintiliae, quantum gaudet amore tuo.*

96

If our grief can bring any pleasure
or comfort to the silent grave,
Calvus—or the longing which
revives in us old loves
and makes us weep for friendships
lost long ago—then surely
Quintilia's less unhappy
about having died so young
than she's comforted by your love.

97

I swear, it's difficult to tell,
by sniffing, which is Aemilius'
mouth and which is his tail.
Neither is cleaner or dirtier
than the other—or rather
his ass-hole's the cleaner and better
of the two—it hasn't any teeth.
His mouth has half a yard of them,
and gums that look exactly
like an old wagon-box.
And besides, it's always gaping
as wide as a mule's cunt
when it's pissing in hot weather.
He screws all the girls he can find
and makes himself out a charmer,
and somehow he's managed to escape
being sent to the grinding-mill
and donkey's work. But the girl
who'd touch him would be willing
to lick the scrofulous backsides
of the public executioner.

98

You're the one, stinking Victius,
if any, of whom we can say
what they say about blabbermouths
and idiots. With that tongue
of yours, if you're given a chance,
you could lick the boots and backsides
of any clodhopper. If you want
to kill us all off, altogether,
just open your mouth, Victius,
and you'll get your wish, for sure.

99

I snatched a kiss from you,
honey-sweet Juventius,
while you were playing—a kiss
sweeter than sweet ambrosia.
But not without being punished.
For more than an hour, I remember,
I hung from the cross, while I tried
to excuse myself to you
but couldn't, with all my tears,
take away the least bit of your anger.
As soon as I'd done it, you washed
your lips with water many times
and rubbed at them with your knuckles
so that no contamination
from my mouth would stay on them—
as though it were the filthy spit
of some prostitute. And what's more,
you turned me over immediately,
unhappy as I was, to cruel Love,
till my kiss turned from ambrosia
to bitterer than bitter gall.
Since this is the way you punish
my unhappy love, I'll never
try snatching kisses anymore.

CI

MVLTAS per gentes et multa per aequora vectus
  advenio has miseras, frater, ad inferias,
ut te postremo donarem munere mortis
  et mutam nequiquam alloquerer cinerem,
quandoquidem fortuna mihi tete abstulit ipsum,
  heu miser indigne frater adempte mihi.
nunc tamen interea haec, prisco quae more parentum
  tradita sunt tristi munere ad inferias,
accipe fraterno multum manantia fletu,
  atque in perpetuum, frater, ave atque vale.

100

Caelius and Quintius,
the flower of Verona's young men,
are desperately in love—
one with Aufilenus, the brother,
the other with his sister Aufilena.
Here, according to the proverb,
is true brotherly love!

Who'll get my blessing? Caelius,
it's you. It was you who showed me
the rarest friendship, tried by fire,
when that violent burning seared me
to the bone. Good luck, Caelius.
I hope you'll be happy with your love.

101

I have come through many countries
and over many seas, brother,
to this unhappy funeral—
to give you the last gifts
of death and speak, though in vain,
to your silent ashes, since fate
has taken your real self from me.
O my poor brother, taken
away from me so suddenly!
Now take these unhappy gifts,
watered with a brother's tears,
which according to the custom
of our fathers are prescribed
for funerals. And forever,
greetings, brother, and farewell.

102

If anything was ever confided
in secret by a trusting friend
to another whose heart was known
to be trustworthy and true,
you'll find me too, Cornelius,
bound by their oath, to become
a regular Harpocrates.

103

Make up your mind, Silo,
if you please. Just give me back
my ten thousand sesterces and then
be as overbearing and rude
as you like. Or else, if you can't
bear to part with all that money,
keep on with your pimping, but please—
not so rude and overbearing.

104

Do you really think I'd be capable
of saying such nasty things
about her who's my very life—
more precious to me than my eyes?
I couldn't do it. How could I,
when I love her so desperately?
But you and that fellow Tappo—
you're capable of anything.

105

Mentula tries to climb Mount Pipleus,
but the Muses drive him down,
head over heels, with little pitchforks.

106

When you see a pretty boy
walking around with a salesman,
what are you supposed to think
except that he's for sale?

107

If anything good ever happens
when you've longed for it but never
dared hope for it, that's real pleasure
for the soul. And that's the reason
it's such a delight (more precious
than gold) that you've come back
to me, Lesbia, my darling,
when I longed for you without hope.
You've come back of your own free will!
This is a day to be marked
with a whiter stone. Who is there
alive that's luckier than I?
Or who can say there's anything
in life more blessed than this?

108

If your white old age, Cominius,
disgraced by your filthy behavior,
should be brought to a sudden close
by the popular will, I've no doubt
that first that tongue of yours
(the enemy of all good things)
would be cut out and given
to a gluttonous vulture. And a crow
would gulp your gouged-out eyes
down his black throat. And dogs
would devour your guts. And wolves
eat up your other parts.

109

You promise me that our love
will be happy, darling, and last
forever, on both sides.
Mighty gods, grant that she'll be able
to keep her promise truly
and really mean what she says
from the heart, so we'll be allowed
to carry through a whole lifetime
this eternal pact of holy love.

110

Aufilena, honest mistresses
are always praised. They collect
their fee for what they've agreed
to do. But you're not honest.
You made promises to me and broke them.
You take but you won't give—
a dirty way of doing things.
To do it would have been honest,
or not to promise, chaste.
But to take all you can get
and cheat on your obligation
is worse than the greediest whore
who puts her body up for sale.

111

Aufilena, to live happily
with one man is the highest praise
of all praises for a married girl.
But it's better to sleep with anyone
anywhere than become the mother
of your own first cousins.

112

You're a great guy, Naso,
and he's a great guy too—
that fellow who goes walking
down to the Forum with you—
I don't think. You're a great guy,
Naso—and a prize pervert.

113

During Pompey's first consulship,
Cinna, there were two who shared
Maecilia's favors. And now
that he's consul again, the two
are still there, but several thousand
have been added to each one.
Adultery breeds adultery.

114

What they say about Mentula
isn't untrue—that he's rich
in property around Firmum
that's stocked with so many fine things:
all kinds of fowling, and fish,
and meadows and plowland and game.
But what of it? He spends more
than it brings him. He's rich, all right,
and poor at the same time.
Let's grant his comfortable acres,
but the man himself is flat broke.

CXVI

SAEPE tibi studioso animo venante requirens
    carmina uti possem mittere Battiadae,
qui te lenirem nobis, neu conarere
    telis infesta mittere in usque caput,
hunc video mihi nunc frustra sumptum esse laborem,
    Gelli, nec nostras hic valuisse preces.
contra nos tela ista tua evitamus amictu:
    at fixus nostris tu dabi supplicium.

115

Mentula has something like thirty
acres of meadow, and forty
of plowland. The rest is swampland.
How can he fail to be richer
than Croesus, when he owns so many
kinds of things in one estate:
pasture, cropland, large woods,
and salt marshes, stretching away
as far as the Hyperboreans
and the great Ocean itself?
All this is wonderful,
but the greatest wonder of all
is the fellow himself—not a man,
at all, really, but a huge
menacing lump of lechery.

116

I've asked myself many times
in my eager, searching mind
how I might send you some poems
of Callimachus, to make you
a little more friendly to me
(and so that you wouldn't try
to send your poisoned darts flying
at my head). But now I see
that my efforts were useless, Gellius,
and my prayers to that effect
accomplished nothing. Instead,
I'll ward off your missiles with my cloak,
but you'll get the punishment
you deserve—transfixed by mine.

This book was set in Linotype Caslon, an old-style type face designed in Britain in 1722. It was printed on 60 lb. Warren's Olde Style Antique Stock at C. E. Pauley and Company, Inc., Indianapolis, and bound by the Heckman Bindery, North Manchester, Ind. Sketches by Iola J. Mills.